The Demons of Liberal Democracy

The Demons of
Liberal Democracy

———

Adrian Pabst

polity

First published in 2019 by Polity Press

Polity Press
65 Bridge Street
Cambridge CB2 1UR, UK

Polity Press
101 Station Landing
Suite 300
Medford, MA 02155, USA

ISBN-13: 978-1-5095-2844-8
ISBN-13: 978-1-5095-2845-5 (pb)

A catalogue record for this book is available from the British Library.

Typeset in 11 on 14 pt Sabon by
Servis Filmsetting Ltd, Stockport, Cheshire
Printed and bound in the United Kingdom by Clays Ltd, Elcograph S.p.A.

For further information on Polity, visit our website: politybooks.com

Contents

Acknowledgements

I was encouraged to write this book by George Owers, and I owe him and his colleagues a debt of gratitude for publishing it with Polity Press. The manuscript was mostly written during my research sabbatical in the academic year 2017–18, and I am grateful to the University of Kent for the opportunity.

My colleagues in the School of Politics and International Relations have been very supportive in my years at Kent, especially Iain MacKenzie, Luca Mavelli, Seán Molloy, Stefan Rossbach, Richard Sakwa, Harmonie Toros and Richard Whitman, as well as Diane Arthurs and Siobhan Dumphy. I have learned much from the students who took my modules 'Market-States and Post-Democracy' and 'Resistance and Alternative to Capitalism', as well as my PhD students Zachary Paikin, Andrew Morris and Paolo Santori.

Earlier versions of some of the chapters were presented at various conferences and workshops. Chapter 1 grew out of a paper I gave at a conference at Durham University in June 2014 entitled 'Post-Democracy, Ten Years On', about the eponymous book by Colin Crouch

Acknowledgements

that first kindled my interest in the self-erosion of liberal democracy. An abridged version was published in *Political Quarterly*, 87/1 (2016), pp. 91–5, and chapter 1 is an extensively revised and expanded version. Chapter 2 was presented at an ESRC-funded workshop on 'Civil Society & Democracy in the Economic Arena' at City University in December 2017. Chapter 3 is based on a keynote address I delivered at the Johns Hopkins Center in Bologna in December 2016. Chapter 4 was first given as a paper to the Conway Hall Ethical Society on 19 February 2017. And chapter 5 is based on my paper given at a workshop on 7 November 2017 on 'Democracy and Human Dignity', hosted jointly by the Las Casas Institute in the University of Oxford, St Mary's University Twickenham and Theos think-tank. I would like to thank the organisers and participants for their comments and suggestions that have helped me to develop my thinking.

My intellectual debts are too numerous to mention, but I would like to acknowledge conversations over many years with close friends and colleagues, including Richard Beardsworth, Russell Berman, Luigino Bruni, Christopher Coker, Jon Cruddas MP, Maurice Glasman, Tim Luke, John Milbank, James Noyes, Marcia Pally, David Pan, the late Nicholas Rengger, Jonathan Rutherford, Roberto Scazzieri, Larry Siedentop, and Stefano and Vera Zamagni.

In recent times, I have benefited much from conversations with Michael Casey, Jason Cowley, Paul Embery, Damien Freeman, Brian Griffith, Jack Hutchison, Ron Ivy, Jim McMahon MP, Morgan McSweeney, Shabana Mahmood MP, Lisa Nandy MP, Jesse Norman MP, Julien O'Connell, Hannah O'Rourke, Steve Reed MP,

Acknowledgements

Rachel Reeves MP, Barbara Ridpath, David Rouch, Michael Sandel, Roger Scruton, Matthew Sowemimo, Liam Stokes and Florence Sutcliffe-Braithwaite.

My greatest debt is to my parents, Reinhart and Brigitte, and it is to them that I dedicate this book.

Introduction – Liberal Democracy in Question

A new narrative is taking hold among the West's ruling elites in politics and the media. The argument is that Western liberal democracies face an existential threat from foreign autocracies and dictatorships, most of all Moscow's propagandist cyber-campaign and electoral interference as part of the Kremlin's hybrid war. Key to this is the claim that social media manipulation swung the result of narrow votes in favour of Brexit and Donald Trump. This seems to be illustrated by Cambridge Analytica, which allegedly bought access to personal data on Facebook in order to micro-target swing voters and those it might have considered to be 'easily persuadable people'. Unable to comprehend the political insurgency that is sweeping through the West, many politicians and pundits appear to believe that millions of their fellow citizens voted against the ruling establishment because Russian bots and data-powered political ads manipulated them.[1] This narrative forgets that our age of anger has its origins in the moral bankruptcy afflicting Western capitalism and the failure of liberal democratic systems to deal with the popular backlash against rapid cultural change. Elites left, right and centre are struggling to grasp why a popular majority rejects the status quo.

Many of those who consider the upheaval shaking Western liberal democracies as fundamentally home-grown tend to view it in primarily economic terms. Once confined to the political fringe, far-left and radical-right insurgents are apparently in the ascendancy because of mounting rage against an establishment that has failed to address the main economic problems, including financial disruption, exorbitant executive pay, youth unemployment and growing regional inequalities. Emblematic of this is all the talk about those 'left behind' by globalisation and about the retreat of liberalism.[2] 2016 was the year when the ghosts of capitalism came back to haunt the elites. For the first time since the Great Depression and the post-war settlement, Brexit and Trump gave the economic losers a political victory over the winners. The popular revolt against the establishment is only beginning, but it has already buried once and for all the idea that Western liberal democracy ushered in the 'end of history' – the conceit that the West's brand of democratic capitalism is the only valid model because it combines political freedom with economic opportunity and social cohesion.

However, it was not just their marginalisation in the economy that voters resented. The fact that they voted against their economic self-interest suggests that their revulsion was to do with the denigration of their values and identities by the members of the professional political class. Hillary Clinton's dismissal of half of Trump voters – many former Democrat supporters – as a 'basket of deplorables' exemplifies the contempt in which liberal elites hold those for whom global free trade, mass immigration and the priority of minority values over declining majorities and their ways of life mean greater economic hardship and unnerving cultural compromises.[3] The elites used to say 'it's the economy, stupid', but now cultural loss appears to trump economic pain.

Liberal democracy is in question because, so far, it has not coped with the economic injustice and divisions in society that threaten the social contract between the people and their representatives. The depth of divisions has been laid bare in recent referendums and elections, as countries are split between young and old, between the metropolis and the provinces, between cities, small towns and the countryside, and between those who are university educated and those who are not. These divisions can be mapped on to the electoral divide of Remain/Brexit, Clinton/Trump and Macron/Le Pen. The old opposition of left/right seems increasingly obsolete, its dominance in contemporary politics superseded by a new narrative of a clash between liberal-cosmopolitan 'people from nowhere' and conservative-communitarian 'people from somewhere'.[4]

Yet this narrative risks substituting one binary world for another – one in which the main fault lines are cultural and generational, encapsulated by the networked metropolitan youth versus the old 'left behind'. Categories of this sort fail to capture the complex composition of urban and suburban communities as well as the dynamics of inequality within them. Simplistic stories about a bright cosmopolitan future or a backlash against globalisation do little to integrate culture and age with class, geography and the economy. We are witnessing the failure of dualistic thinking, and this will not be resolved by substituting one binary for another.

Nor does it help to add the prefix 'post'. Post-capitalism or post-liberalism accord too much importance to that which they aim at overcoming, and they fail to name alternatives anchored in reality. This flaw was always present in post-modernism and cognate concepts, which were mostly intensifications of certain Enlightenment strands in modernity, such as the cult of the individual, the sovereign will (individual or collective) and the power of techno-science to liberate us not simply from the trap of capitalist markets but also from any limits of nature or history.[5] These and other assumptions are disintegrating in the form of the destruction of the person by individualism, the submission to technology and the erosion of society by online friendships and virtual community that are abstracted from real relationships.

Underpinning this disintegration are the forces of dispossession unleashed by liberalism, which include capitalism, statism and globalisation. All of them involve a shift from the self-government of citizens towards the administration of things and the governance by numbers.[6] Both people and nature are reduced to commodities circulating in an unmediated space based on an oscillation between the individual who is disembedded from history, institutions and relationships, on the one hand, and the collective grounded in a positivist legal system, on the other. This liberal order is inherently unstable because liberalism erodes the very foundations on which it rests.[7] It brings about economic injustice and divisions in society that are threatening the social contract between the people and their representatives, which is the bedrock of the liberal tradition. The liberal elites fail to understand that the anti-establishment insurgents are a consequence, not the cause, of the failure of liberalism.

Liberalism is a slippery term with many meanings. In this book I argue that the liberalism which has failed is not the whole liberal tradition but, rather, a contemporary radicalisation of specific ideals, in particular (1) freedom without social solidarity (going back to John Locke and Immanuel Kant); (2) the primacy of the individual underwritten by the collective power of the state over civic associations (going back to Thomas Hobbes and Jean-Jacques Rousseau); and (3) faith in a better future underpinned by a secular metaphysics of progress (going back to Auguste Comte and J. S. Mill).[8] Three notable exceptions are the constitutionalist liberalism of Edmund Burke and Alexis de Tocqueville, the social liberalism of Benjamin Constant and François Guizot, and the new liberalism of T. H. Green, L. T. Hobhouse and J. A. Hobson, with its emphasis on the conditions of individual flourishing sustained by networks of mutual assistance.[9]

By contrast with these three strands, contemporary liberals defend a negative conception of freedom as absence of constraints on individual choice (except the law and private conscience). The liberal accentuation of 'negative' freedom rather than substantive shared ends informs ideals such as emancipation, self-expression and choice. Contemporary liberals also advance an economic and social individualism that is promoted by government and the law. This liberal priority of the individual over groups has led to the preference for state and market mechanisms over the intermediary institutions of civil society. Moreover, contemporary liberals have doubled down and embraced what John Gray calls hyper-liberalism.[10] Far from defending tolerance and a richer conception of freedom, hyper-liberal politics seeks to overcome any attachment to national and group identity in favour of a borderless world without restrictions on personal choice. Gone is a commitment to critical debate about rival values and beliefs, combined with a concern for truth. Hyper-liberals at best are indifferent to facts that contradict their belief in progress and at worst engage in sophistry with virtue-signalling self-righteousness. They condemn patriotism as reactionary and national identity as a repressive construction while promoting a cosmopolitan vision that is remote from the everyday existence of most people.

Gray is right to suggest that hyper-liberalism is less a departure from the main liberal tradition than an intensification of liberalism as a secular religion. With a blind faith in progress and individual emancipation from all forms of shared belonging, liberalism at the hands of Mill, who was deeply influenced by the positivist philosophy of Comte,[11] became a new religion of humanity that ignores people's yearning for security and meaning. Beyond Gray, I argue that liberalism cannot comprehend popular attachment to relationships embedded in civic institutions – from the local parish and town hall to the armed forces and parliament. It equates such sentiments with atavistic prejudice that must be swept away in the name of progress embodied in transnational state power and the expanding global market. Secular progressive liberalism flips over into large-scale social engineering to refashion society in its own image, combining free-market fundamentalism with social egalitarianism and individualised identity politics.

Under the influence of this creed, liberal democracy is increasingly illiberal and undemocratic.[12] Since antiquity, philosophers have cautioned against the slide of democracy into oligarchy, demagogy, anarchy and tyranny. Today this warning applies to liberalism and the dangers it poses to democratic rule. In the final instance, different liberal democratic models are self-eroding as they descend into oligarchical rule, demagogic manipulation, an anarchic fragmentation of society, and what Tocqueville called the 'tyranny of voluntary servitude' – a 'kind of servitude, ordered, mild and peaceable . . ., a singular power, tutelary, all-encompassing'.[13] Those demons of liberal democracy are perhaps irrepressible but they can be tamed. A genuine democracy tries to reconcile estranged interests in a negotiated settlement based on leadership and popular participation. This involves the forging of a common life around shared principles and practices that seek to balance freedom with fraternity, equality with reciprocity, and tradition with modernity.

The dignity of the person involves both liberty and fraternal relations of belonging to communities and civic institutions – such as schools, hospitals, railways, water companies, post offices and housing associations – that generate a sense of connection and loyalty. Where they serve people's needs and interests, they are a good in their lives and a source of social bonds and collective action. Democracy requires a culture of shared norms that nurtures a shared sense of affection and attachment. Such norms include a balance of equality before the law with reciprocal obligation – duties we owe to ourselves and to others. In a democracy we have precious individual rights but also duties to care for others

7

and for their well-being as well as to lead by example. Reciprocity is about relationships of give-and-receive, contribution and reward, on which democracy depends for trust and cooperation that cannot be mandated by law or instituted by economic contract alone.

A democratic politics also has to recognise that we are social beings who are partially constituted by an inheritance of language, relationships, place and belief, which needs to be conserved and renewed. By trying to hold the balance between tradition and modernity, democracy is as conservative as it is radical. These and other principles underpin common values of hard work, family, community, country and international solidarity. Such a democratic renewal requires a political debate shaped by a public philosophy – one that can address deeper divisions around questions of shared meaning and belonging. That is the central argument of this book.

Each chapter combines a critique of contemporary liberal democracy with ideas for democratic renewal. Chapter 1 shows how the tendency of the liberal establishment towards oligarchy and technocratic rule legitimates the invocation of the 'will of the people', which at the hands of the insurgents often becomes debased and descends into mob rule.[14] Liberalism and populism polarise politics and undermine parliamentary democracy just when democracy needs a transcendent conversation about what people share as citizens – what binds them together as members of national and cultural communities. Chapter 2 argues that liberalism has become an engine of oligarchy instead of open markets, as exemplified by the monopoly power of tech giants and global finance. The alternative approach is not simply better regulation but a much more fundamental change of ownership and internal company ethos that gives workers power as part of an economic democracy we have never built.

Chapter 3 shows how contemporary liberalism is a catalyst for demagogy and employs similar manipulative methods to populism. Democratic renewal will have to include a politics committed to proper debate in search of substantive truths. Chapter 4 argues that liberalism's erosion of social bonds and civic ties has led to the fragmentation of society and anarchy, which will require new forms of solidarity to balance individual freedoms and the promotion of reciprocity to mitigate selfish individualism. Chapter 5 suggests that the liberal drift towards oligarchy, demagogy and anarchy erodes the principles and practices of liberality – free speech, free inquiry, tolerance – on which a vibrant democracy depends. In this manner contemporary liberalism brings about Tocqueville's tyranny of voluntary servitude. The alternative this book puts forward is a radical renewal of democracy anchored in people associating around shared interests and building intermediary institutions that provide agency and meaning.

1

Democracy between Liberalism and Populism

1 The retreat of (liberal) democracy

Democracy is in retreat. After spreading from the 1970s onwards, the last decade or so has seen democratic setbacks around the world. Various indices, such as Freedom House's annual report and *The Economist*'s Democracy Index, suggest that countries that saw a decline in democracy outnumbered those that registered gains for twelve consecutive years.[1] New democracies that in the 1990s and early 2000s seemed promising success stories – including Turkey and Venezuela – are sliding into elective dictatorships. Meanwhile old democracies are flawed even as their governments and media often lecture others on the dangers of rolling back democratic norms, as in the case of EU measures (supported by Germany and France) to censure Poland and Hungary.

Barely a quarter of a century after the 'end of history', the prospect of a global convergence towards Western liberal market democracy seems remote. Instead, the discourse has shifted to notions of 'democratic recession', which is reinforced by the argument that the loss of belief in democracy among especially younger citizens in the West is evidence of a 'democratic disconnect' and the 'deconsolidation of democracy'.[2] However, long-term studies of social attitudes towards democratic systems of governments, such as the World Values Survey, suggest that popular support for democracy is growing stronger, not weaker, and that the moral values on which younger people base their democratic beliefs have turned significantly more liberal over time.[3] Although both the empirical evidence and the underlying theoretical premises remain a matter of fierce debate, there is little doubt that the expectation in 1989 – democracy deepens where it already exists and spreads to countries where it was previously suppressed – has not come to pass.

The post-Cold War order is unravelling and with it the supposed triumph of liberal democracy over all other political models. Instead, one-party state capitalism is rivalling multi-party market capitalism, as Beijing promotes 'socialism with Chinese characteristics', which is in reality a fusion of communist politics with neo-liberal economics that is faithful to the Leninist promise to replace 'the government of people' with 'the administration of things'. This is part of a wider trend away from democratisation towards an authoritarian consolidation of power by ruling parties and strongmen in countries as varied as Russia, Turkey, Egypt, the Philippines and, to some extent, India and Japan – all of which are closely integrated with the world economy. But the old assumption that economic liberalisation and a growing middle class would usher in political freedom and a peaceful transition to democratic pluralism no longer holds either. Outside the liberal West, it seems that the middle class favours state provision of public goods over market competition and national leadership over democratic participation. This 'new understanding of the middle class calls into question predictions that powerful authoritarian states like China will eventually democratise.'[4]

Moreover, non-Western countries reject Western liberal democracy because it seems to be associated with political weakness, economic instability and social division. Liberal forms of representative government are breaking down under the weight of a dysfunctional party system and the power of special interests, as multinational corporations capture states and limit their ability to provide public services. Growing interdependence has exacerbated the volatility of economies that are increasingly dominated by financialised capitalism. Mass migration, weak demographic growth and multiculturalism have eroded civic bonds and left Western societies more atomised. Taken together, these factors undermine the legitimacy of Western democratic rule in the eyes of the non-West and cast doubt over who composes and controls the supposedly sovereign demos.

The worldwide revolt against liberal democracy is also engulfing the West, as illustrated by the Brexit vote, the election of Donald Trump, the strong support for the Front National (now renamed as Rassemblement National), the AfD's presence in the German parliament, Italy's majority vote for anti-establishment parties, and the rise of far-left and far-right forces elsewhere in Europe. Popular support for this political insurgency marks a repudiation of the liberal idea of global progress towards peace and prosperity.[5] Gone is the post-war promise of progress for every generation. According to a study by the Pew Research Center in December 2015, the American middle class, once the largest class and the very embodiment of the 'American Dream', is the majority no longer. The USA is increasingly divided along both socio-economic and cultural class lines, with the middle being hollowed out. Growing numbers slide into poverty and precariousness, while the top 20 per cent monopolise access to good-quality education, housing, health care and jobs.[6]

Falling levels of social mobility extend to Britain, where the government's social mobility commission found in its last two reports on the annual 'state of the nation' that the millennials are the first cohort since 1945 to start their career on lower incomes than their parents and that downward mobility has reached levels not seen since the 1920s. In France and Germany, market fundamentalism is less rampant, but their respective political systems struggle to address the economic and cultural insecurity of a majority.[7] Emmanuel Macron and Angela Merkel's defence of liberal democracy against its adversaries cannot mask the growing gap between political parties and the people they purport to represent – including new ones such as La République en Marche that pretend to reconnect civil society to politics in a spirit of direct democracy but, so far, are little more than top-down orchestrations to propel their leaders into power and maintain a personality cult.

Linked to this is the problem of 'double delegation', whereby representatives elected by citizens delegate power to unelected officials who are part of a professional political class.[8] A governing elite that is seen as out of touch breeds disillusionment and cynicism among voters who are increasingly disengaged, leaving a void that is filled by the contest between the establishment and anti-elite insurgents, which further amplifies the sense of popular alienation. Contemporary liberal democracy is caught in a downward spiral that undermines its claim to legitimate rule – decisive leadership that learns the lessons of past mistakes, combined with popular consent for elected representatives and their decisions. The tendency to muddle through and repeat the error of not tackling widespread concerns about economic justice or social solidarity means that the liberal democratic system of government faces a lack of legitimacy. If the liberal system has endured and seems resilient, it is to do with liberalism's fusion of the power of coercion with the power of dissuasion – dissent is tolerated insofar as it is directed at the enemies of liberalism who are portrayed as illegitimate. Their criticism is dismissed as reactionary and therefore invalid, which reveals the illiberal core of contemporary liberals.

2 *Conceptualising the crisis*

Three kinds of response to the retreat of liberal democracy can be distinguished. The first is to blame authoritarian populists at home and abroad who are apparently intent on subverting open societies, democratic government and Western ways of life. The assertion is that a new Populist International led by Moscow thinks of itself as a revolutionary vanguard that hates the liberal West and seeks to destroy democratic institutions in the name of defending the true Western civilisation against the supposedly existential threat of 'Islamisation'.[9] The second response is to suggest that the problem with liberal democracy is not its values but its failure to deliver on its promise of freedom, openness and equality. Only liberal democratic government, so the argument goes, can secure well-being, stability, peace, fundamental rights and liberties.[10] Both responses call on the defenders of liberal democracy to stop being complacent and to engage once more in the global battle of ideas.

The third response differs insofar as it focuses on the foundations of liberal democracy in a way that the other two do not. From this perspective, the current crisis is not new but an intensification of some long-standing developments that have led to a mutation of democratic rule. This has been conceptualised in terms of 'post-democracy', 'the specter of inverted totalitarianism' and the 'hollowing out' of democratic politics.[11] Connecting these concepts is the idea that the post-war period of democratisation has given way to a concentration of power in the hands of small groups that are unrepresentative and unaccountable, as exemplified by the nexus between global firms and national governments, which changes the very nature of democracy. And when elected demagogues such as Silvio Berlusconi or Donald Trump begin to subvert democratic institutions, democracies can disappear even as formal procedures remain in place.[12] Therefore the task of renewing democracy goes much further than confronting external threats or fixing domestic policy.

In what follows, my argument is that post-democracy and cognate concepts do not capture a more fundamental pattern – the inherent tendency of liberal democracy to descend into oligarchy, demagogy and anarchy: first of all, the rise of a new oligarchical class that wields power over parliament and the people; second, the resurgence of demagogic politics linked to the manipulation of public debate by ruling elites and insurgents – for example, supposedly enlightened elites armed with technocratic facts versus apparently fake news peddled by those defending the 'will of the people'; and, third, the emergence of anarchic society connected with the fragmentation of everyday life and a weakening of civic bonds. In consequence, liberal democracy risks sliding into a system that maintains the illusion of free choice while generating Tocqueville's tyranny of voluntary servitude.

The argument is not that democracy is the same as dictatorship but, rather, that over time liberal democracy becomes illiberal and undemocratic precisely because it is compatible with oligarchic, demagogic and anarchic elements. A new oligarchy seeks to centralise power, concentrate wealth and manipulate public opinion by using media spin, closing down debate and ironing out plurality. Its members' aim is to entrench a system to which 'there is no alternative' (Margaret Thatcher). Thus the process whereby democratic rule becomes debased and even 'despotic' encompasses a series of mutations within democracy itself. Among others, these include elected representatives and governments that act as an interested, self-serving party; a corporate capture of the state and the economy; a demobilisation of the citizenry; a cult of abstract equality; and a retreat into the individualised identity of minority groups that excludes a majority from mainstream politics and has nothing to say about what people have in common.[13] Identity liberalism has reinforced the rise of a political insurgency against the ruling elites, both of

16

which undermine democracy in different ways, and it is therefore this insurgency that the chapter now explores.

3 Authoritarianism, populism, liberalism

Many members of the liberal elites believe that their political rivals are authoritarian populists who want to bring down the EU, reverse globalisation and abolish democracy. But the problem with terms such as 'authoritarian' or 'populist' is that they can apply to liberals just as much as to their far-left or radical-right challengers. Authoritarianism is often a method that governing parties across the political spectrum have used to ride roughshod over parliament and to curtail civil liberties. Populism in the sense of vote-winning manipulation of the electorate has never been the monopoly of anti-elite insurgents. Liberals on the centre-left and the centre-right of politics who complain about populists forget their own role in the rise of today's political insurgency.

At first liberals fused politics with public relations and circumvented parliamentary democracy in favour of direct communication with the people mediated since the Thatcher government and the Reagan administration mostly by the Murdoch media. Following Bill Clinton's New Democrats, neo-liberal populism mutated into the 'corporate populism' of New Labour's culture of spin that was taken to the next level in the 2015 general election, and particularly the EU referendum, by George Osborne's Project Fear.[14] For some time, corporate populism won, but in the end it was roundly repudiated by voters who no longer trust the liberal centre. The Brexit vote, Trump's election and mass support for the far-left

17

politics of Greece's Syriza, Spain's Podemos, Jean-Luc Mélenchon's La France Insoumise, Bernie Sanders and Jeremy Corbyn mark a popular revolt against the manipulative populism of liberal elites. At the same time, Berlusconi and now Trump embody an anti-liberal version of corporate populism. It is an ambiguous moment because it deepens divisions while also opening up the space for a renewed democratic contest between rival ideologies rather than the four-decade-long convergence towards centrist liberalism.[15]

Those liberals who are in power are adopting a strategy of co-opting populism that will either defeat or strengthen the insurgents but in any case moves politics in a more demagogic direction. Emmanuel Macron, who is an establishment insurgent, stormed to the French presidency on the back of an ultra-liberal programme of greater European integration, economic modernisation and multiculturalism. But he did so based on a populist campaign that included a personal political movement, En Marche (bearing his initials), an attack on the mainstream parties, and a promise of both left- and right-wing policies. Since his election he has governed partly like a populist by being tough on immigration and projecting the image of a charismatic leader – with a cult of Jupiter that is reminiscent more of the Roman Empire than of the French Republic, but perhaps just a curious mix of Napoleon with de Gaulle.

By contrast, Angela Merkel – Europe's other liberal leader – has chosen to resist populism by pursuing another grand coalition between the CDU and the SPD, which both suffered heavy losses in the 2017 election. Such a coalition will likely reinforce the 'social democratisation' of the Christian Democrats and the 'neo-liberalisation' of the Social Democrats, which helped to provoke the rise of the populist AfD (Alternative für Deutschland) in the first place. Whether the strategy is to co-opt or to resist populism, both Macron and Merkel project themselves as defenders of liberal democracy and a resurgent EU against the rising tide of Euroscepticism on which the anti-establishment insurgents of the radical right and the hard left thrive.[16]

The label 'populist' is used for political movements with mass support for ideas of which liberal elites disapprove. Populists in Central and Eastern Europe, such as the Hungarian prime minister Viktor Orbán or the governing Law and Justice Party in Poland, reject the liberal orthodoxy of free-market globalisation, supranational governance, mass immigration and cosmopolitan identity in favour of state intervention in the economy, national sovereignty, controlled migration and the protection of traditional culture. Their position is paradoxical in the sense that they portray their politics as anti-EU but pro-European, fiscally conservative but economically egalitarian, and against liberalism but on the side of democracy. As Tibor Fischer – whose parents were Hungarian refugees from communism – has argued, Orbán's talk of 'illiberal democracy' is primarily a rejection of left-wing social liberalism and not an all-out attack on Hungarian democracy as such.[17] Under Orbán, Fischer claims, Hungary continues to have party competition, competitive elections, a plural media, independent courts, a functioning parliament and the rule of law.

Yet, at the same time as the formal institutions remain in place, the substance of democratic politics is being hollowed out in the sense that Orbán has adopted the rhetoric and ideology of far-right movements such as Jobbik, combining ethno-nationalism and the demonisation of immigrants with campaigns that have strong anti-Semitic undertones. Similarly, the governing Law and Justice Party in Poland has not abolished altogether the separation of powers or the constitutional checks and balances, but it is seeking an ideological capture of public media, state corporations and the judiciary, as well as taking steps to rewrite the history of Polish involvement in the Holocaust in a way that could provide licence for anti-Semitism. In each case, the governments of Hungary and Poland are creating a climate of suspicion and intimidation of political opponents, who are often branded as enemies of 'the People' – a favourite term of Trump and hard-core Brexiteers.

For these reasons, contemporary populism cannot simply be described as democratic. Flourishing democracies depend not just on functioning formal constitutions but also on informal shared norms. Opponents are legitimate adversaries in a political contest, not illegitimate enemies who should be locked up – as Trump demanded in relation to 'Crooked Hillary'. The democratic process requires the pursuit of truth based on evidence and balanced judgement, not on naked appeals to lies or bigotry. Both ruling liberal elites and anti-liberal insurgents have undermined those norms, as elections descend into a choice between rival conspiracy theories, deception and vilification. Clinton's above-mentioned jibe about half of Trump supporters being a 'basket of deplorables' is no less undemocratic than Trump's legitimation of racial stereotyping and racial preference.

Anti-establishment insurgents also argue for a different conception of the EU, which they claim has echoes of Europe's more authentic traditions – the nation, the family, the Christian legacy, prudential politics and majoritarian democracy.[18] Arguably, popular opinion in many Western European countries is to some extent moving in this direction, as the mainstream centre-left and centre-right has either been defeated or is being pushed by populist parties that are defending national interests against perceived or real encroachments from Brussels. As Cas Mudde and Cristóbal Rovira Kaltwasser write, 'in a world that is dominated by democracy and liberalism, populism has essentially become an illiberal democratic response to undemocratic liberalism. Populists ask uncomfortable questions about undemocratic aspects of liberal institutions and policies',[19] including questions about globalisation, immigration and identity that have been dismissed by liberal elites. And, in response to populist movements, establishment liberals resort to the kind of corporate populism that deploys demagogic tactics in an attempt to regain majority support, which further divides society and polarises politics. This is not at all to suggest that, once elected, anti-establishment insurgents become ardent defenders of popular democracy. On the contrary, they often try to override constitutional limits on their power in ways that change the character and substance of democratic institutions. This, as I shall argue below, is an endemic tendency of representative democracy, of which both liberal elites and anti-establishment insurgents take advantage.

But to dismiss insurgents as 'demagogic' implies that they lack any legitimacy compared with the supposedly respectable politics of the liberal left and right. As the French philosopher Pierre Manent has remarked, liberal democracy in its current configuration favours a competition for power between what he calls 'populist demagogy' and the 'fanaticism of the centre'.[20] This conceptualises the new opposition that has superseded the old left/right divide. But here one can go further than Manent to suggest that both centrists and populists fuel each other in a manner that undermines democratic rule. Anti-liberal insurgents claim to represent the 'will of the people' while disregarding individual rights, minority concerns and constitutional norms underpinning the distribution of power between the executive, the legislature and the judiciary. This insurgency has enlisted mass support due to the failure of illiberal undemocratic liberalism to build an economy that works for all and to reflect the cultural norms of a majority. Anti-liberal insurgents are winning in large part because undemocratic liberals are lacking in political engagement, accountability and trust in their fellow citizens.

Liberals and their opponents erode democracy in ways that are mutually reinforcing. The tendency of the liberal establishment towards oligarchy and technocratic rule legitimates the invocation of the 'will of the people', which at the hands of the insurgents often becomes debased and descends into mob rule. Crucially, both liberalism and the insurgency erode parliamentary democracy and have little to say about what people share in common – civic or cultural identity. Thus the political insurgency sweeping through Western countries is symptomatic of a revolt against liberalism without popular democracy by movements that seek to institute a popular democracy without liberalism.

Contemporary liberal democracy is increasingly illiberal and undemocratic. It has not only adopted but also insulated economic liberalism from accountability by shifting power from the legislature to bureaucratic agencies that make their own laws (also called 'regulations') as well as to trade courts and supranational bodies – none of which are properly accountable to parliament. In office, liberal progressive parties on either side of the political spectrum have reinforced the divide between elites and the institutions they control, on the one hand, and the people and their elected representatives, on the other. Liberalism as an ideology and a system of government has imposed ever greater constraints on democratic majorities by enshrining individual rights and defending certain minority group interests. Just as power has shifted to individuals and sectional groups, so too larger groups and the majority are feeling disenfranchised. Insurgents use populist methods as a means of securing popular backing. As a result, populism is increasingly seen as the lifeblood of majoritarian rule, which changes the character of liberal democracy. Far from being a temporary drift, the tendency towards oligarchy (concentrating power in the hands of unaccountable elites), demagogy (manipulating democratic debate and public opinion) and anarchy (social fragmentation) pervades modern liberal democracy, as the remainder of the chapter suggests.

4 A new oligarchy

A crisis of representation is engulfing Western liberal democracies as diverse as the USA, the UK, Italy, France and Germany. Public trust in political institutions is falling sharply, especially in mainstream political parties that have morphed from mass movements into small elite-dominated organisations.[21] Faced with insurgents, party establishments are perceived to defend their own self-interest and the interests of their donors rather than their voters. The collapse in party membership, coupled with a long-term decline in voter turnout, suggests that popular influence on governing elites is minimal.[22] Moreover, a growing number of elected officials are professional politicians from ever narrower socio-economic backgrounds who are seen as neither connecting with ordinary voters, nor governing in the interest of the majority, nor addressing the long-term needs of society.

This suggests a drift of liberal democracy towards effective oligarchy, which is manifest in the tendency of democratically elected representatives to compose an interested party in itself. Typically, political parties in government tend to tackle issues that concern either their own factional support or the factional support of their opponents, which they may act on in order to outflank them – as with the question of immigration. But governing parties prove relatively impotent when it comes to matters affecting the whole of national or international society, such as the migration crisis, environmental devastation, infrastructure investment or cartel capitalism. This is because, although the neglect of such issues is detrimental to all, they are rarely the most immediate and pressing concern of the group whose vested interest has captured a political party.[23] Individually and collectively, citizens are therefore subject to 'the tyranny of small choices', as when we opt to shop in a chain store for convenience or cheapness, even though we do not really desire to lose independent shops and suffer the consequent decline of local prosperity and solidarity that this often entails. Sustaining a balance of oligarchic interests by representative government for seemingly democratic reasons is increasingly at odds with representing the public interest.

The rise of a new oligarchy is not confined to ruling parties but extends to the executive. Liberal democracy is characterised by the exponential growth of executive legislation (often rubber-stamped by a parliamentary majority beholden to executive writ) and the growing power of the judiciary relative to the legislature. A new supranational class of judges seems unable to resist the temptation either to aggrandise its jurisdictional power or to assist the executive in imposing laws that further concentrate wealth or power. And where the action of judges provides a check on inflated governmental power, it can unwittingly foster a litigious culture that privileges the powerful and wealthy while undermining equal access to justice.

Democratic representation suffers at the hands of the 'judicial aristocracy' because, as Tocqueville pointed out, the latter has a much greater affinity with the executive than with the people and privileges public order over all other considerations: 'the best security of public order is authority. It must not be forgotten that, if they [lawyers] prize the free institutions of their country much, they nevertheless value the legality of those institutions far more: they are less afraid of tyranny than of arbitrary power.'[24] In the USA where, as a result of separating state from church and instituting a civil religion, there is no higher authority than the constitution and its guardians (executive and judiciary), democracy is dominated by what Tocqueville describes as an aristocratic class of magistrates and lawyers who 'form a party which . . .

25

extends over the whole community, and it penetrates into all classes of society; it acts upon the country imperceptibly, but it finally fashions it to suit its purposes.'[25]

The lack of accountability and popular participation is compounded by a process of 'self-corruption' whereby an elected executive claims the legitimate authority to exceed its own mandate in the face of circumstances, which could not be anticipated by that mandate and which the electorate does not vote on. Counter-terrorist legislation following 9/11 that suspends certain civil liberties or the bailing out of both banks and states that transferred debt to the taxpayer are emblematic of this. In each case, governments act predominantly in the interest of small groups, such as the security industry, institutional investors and global bond markets. Arguably, this represents an oligarchic defence of the bases of oligarchic control – whether an emergency response to a threat or an opportunity to extend power (or both at once). Either way, liberal democracy is compatible with an oligarchy that goes well beyond the power of global firms – the focus of the post-democracy thesis.

This oligarchy takes the form of 'old elites' and 'new classes'.[26] The former include political dynasties and captains of industry, while the latter encompass networks such as the 'tech oligarchy' in Silicon Valley, global finance on Wall Street and an array of technocrats in government – among them a new managerial armada of accountants and auditors. Both 'old elites' and 'new classes' use the procedures of representative democracy in order to increase their power, wealth and social status. In this process, an unrepresentative executive – together with a moneyed oligarchy and an overweening judiciary – often ignores the more informal expression of citizens' interests. Chapter 2 will show how oligarchy is pervasive in liberal democracies because liberalism failed to build an effective economic democracy that can distribute power, wealth and social status more widely.

5 A new demagogy

Liberal democracies face the permanent threat of illiberal forces that seek to destroy individual liberties paradoxically in the name of free speech, as in the case of hard-left militants, far-right racist groups or religious fundamentalists. However, liberal democracy itself can be a catalyst for demagogy. First of all, there is the tension between substantive values and procedural standards. A key dilemma facing any democratic system is that it constantly needs to balance two competing demands: respecting majority will and commanding popular consent, on the one hand, and protecting individuals and minorities from oppression, on the other. To do so, democracies have historically tended to combine certain foundational values – such as liberty, equality and fraternity in France, or life, liberty and the pursuit of happiness in the USA – with formal rules and procedures. The problem is that, when rival values clash (say, individual freedom and equality for all), contemporary liberalism suggests that people can only 'agree to disagree' and settle for abstract, formal standards such as ground rules of fairness (as in the political liberalism of John Rawls and Ronald Dworkin).

Such a conception of fairness is based on 'negative liberty' – the absence of constraints on the individual

27

other than the law and private conscience.[27] The principle of negative freedom implies that liberal democracy should promote maximal freedom of choice over any shared substantive ends such as the common good, which can be defined as an ordering of relationships in a way that holds in balance individual fulfilment with mutual flourishing, based on the dignity and equality of all people. The maximisation of negative liberty occurs regardless of whether this conception of liberty undermines the quest for mutual recognition more than for total equality or absolute emancipation. In this manner, the liberal privileging of impartial standards may amount to the imposition of preferences that do not command popular consent and thus cannot be described as genuinely democratic.

Second, the relative liberal indifference to substantive values can reinforce the tendency of liberal democracies to manipulate opinion and exploit fear. Liberal politics claims to guard against illiberal and undemocratic elements: the bigot, the xenophobe and the racist but also the terrorist, the refugee or the welfare-scrounger. In consequence, a purported defence of democracy is itself invoked to justify the suspending of democratic decision-making and civil liberties, as with post-9/11 counter-terrorist legislation that suspended core constitutional provisions and values of liberality: fair detention, fair trial, right to a defence, assumed innocence, *habeas corpus*, good treatment of the convicted, and a measure of free speech and free inquiry – not to mention the surveillance apparatus. Declaring a state of emergency is a constitutive characteristic of modern states, and liberal democracies are no exception when it comes to making exceptional powers permanent.[28]

Liberal democracies can also manipulate opinion, and demagogy is an inevitable consequence of liberalism's primacy of procedure over substance. An ever greater use of techniques derived from public relations and the advertising industry exacerbates the demagogic drift. The 'culture' of spin, media stunts, focus groups and endless electoral campaigns has turned politics into a spectacle of general mass opinion that can be described as a form of manipulative populism. In response to the manipulative populism of the ruling elites, Western democracies witness the periodic emergence of anti-elite populism by insurgent movements – the People's Party in the late nineteenth century or more recently the Tea Party in the USA, post-war Poujadisme and the Front National since the 1970s in France, or the UK Independence Party and Jeremy Corbyn backed by Momentum in Britain. Silvio Berlusconi and now Donald Trump are examples of how billionaires-turned-politicians compete to be the most radical 'outsiders' and smash the party establishment in the process. As the political centre collapses and the old opposition of left versus right becomes obsolete, new groups rise to power in defiance of political laws and in violation of the informal norms underpinning democracy.

Up to a point, the free press and the internet protect democracy against this slide into demagogy. However, despite the participatory potential of social media, the expansion of new technological capabilities enhances both algorithmic self-regulation and remote manipulation.[29] Just because the virtual cyberspace lacks a robust and readily implementable ethos of self-discipline and reciprocal practice, it tends to favour fleeting tastes and a self-referential culture that lends itself to the sort of mass surveillance for ostensibly commercial purposes but in reality is open to the military-industrial complex – as illustrated by the NSA spying scandal and Facebook's alleged dealings with Cambridge Analytica. Liberal institutions have aided in unmasking abuses, but do they promote the courage and strength to confront systematic snooping and protect privacy? Chapter 3 will explore how the tech oligarchy accelerates democracy's descent into demagogy and how democratic politics could be transformed in the direction of pursuing the truth.

6 *A new anarchy*

Liberal democracy has brought about greater freedoms and opportunities by extending individual rights. Inherited status that concentrated power among the aristocracy has been replaced by a constitutionally guaranteed equality before the law. Societies are freer and fairer, especially for women and minorities – though much remains to be done. However, liberal gains also entail losses, in particular the progressive erosion of the social bonds and civic ties on which vibrant democracies depend for trust and cooperation. Democratic politics favours greater equality of opportunity, and for some time it provided rising levels of social mobility, but by the same token it is linked to the fragmentation of society. Paradoxically, democracy – especially under the influence of liberal capitalism – can engender societies that are simultaneously more interdependent and more atomised: as Michael Sandel writes, 'in our public life we are more entangled, but less attached, than ever before.'[30]

Democracy between Liberalism and Populism

More fundamentally, liberal democracy tends to oscillate between the sovereign power of the executive and the sovereign power of citizens as freely choosing individuals who are removed from the constraints of interpersonal relations and who entertain predominantly contractual ties with one another. The problem is that this has the effect of undermining human association and the political role of voluntary, democratically self-governing intermediary institutions such as professional associations, trade unions or universities.[31] Without the mediating function of such institutions, democracy risks mutating into an anarchy of competing individuals who pursue their own self-interest without much regard for reciprocal recognition or mutual benefit. The ensuing conflict is either regulated by the 'invisible hand' of the market or policed by the 'visible hand' of the state – or both at once. The real alternative is not just greater democratic representation but also much stronger elements of participatory and associative democracy at regional and local levels (as chapter 4 sets out).

Ultimately, the primacy of state and market power over human association can lead to a democratic system that instils a sense of voluntary servitude – a form of subtle manipulation by ostensible consent whereby people subject themselves freely to the will of the ruling oligarchy. The institutions of the central administrative state and the global market regulate the 'naturally given' (but in reality merely assumed) anarchy, which is exacerbated by the lack of associative ties. Pierre Manent puts this well: 'democratic man is the freest man to have ever lived and at the same time the most domesticated . . . he can only be granted, he can only give himself, so much liberty because he is so domesticated.'[32] Far from lamenting a lost patriarchy, Manent builds on the work of Tocqueville to critique conformism and the loss of human agency. As Tocqueville anticipated nearly two hundred years ago, liberal democracies that privilege mass opinion and self-interested representatives at the expense of education into virtue and bonds of association can produce forms of tutelary power:

> the supreme power then extends its arm over the whole community. It covers the surface of society with a network of small complicated rules, minute and uniform, through which the most original minds and the most energetic characters cannot penetrate, to rise above the crowd. The will of man is not shattered, but softened, bent, and guided; men are seldom forced by it to act, but they are constantly restrained from acting. Such a power does not destroy, but it prevents existence; it does not tyrannize, but it compresses, enervates, extinguishes, and stupefies a people, till each nation is reduced to nothing better than a flock of timid and industrious animals, of which the government is the shepherd. ... servitude of the regular, quiet, and gentle kind ... might be combined more easily than is commonly believed with some of the outward forms of freedom, and that it might even establish itself under the wing of the sovereignty of the people.[33]

7 Democracy's demons

Liberal democracy is caught between elites and insurgents who fuel each other's illiberal undemocratic tendencies and feed the demons of oligarchy, demagogy, anarchy and tyranny. The renewal of the democratic promise to distribute power, wealth and social status more widely among the people will therefore require something other than 'more liberal democracy' or 'more political insurgency'. It will need the creation or strengthening of popular democratic forms such as citizen assemblies, of civic institutions such as intermediary associations, and also of extra-democratic elements such as the rule of law and a sense of shared mores – a shared horizon of common purpose.

One starting point is people's affection for institutions such as parliaments, independent courts and the free press, as well as attachment to values of work, family, community, country and international solidarity. To bring about a sense of shared purpose demands a better balance between the consent and participation of people, the advice and educative guidance of groups, and the discernment and decisive leadership of decision-makers. In other words, strengthening democracy involves renewing the ancient constitution with its interplay between the sovereignty of the 'one' (the ruler in the sense of the unity of the executive), the 'few' (groups at all levels of society) and the 'many' (the people). The remainder of the book sets out ideas that can help to move in this direction in a context of migration, multiculturalism, the decline of traditional (religious and cultural) values and the rise of rampant individualism underwritten by the state, beginning with economic oligarchy.

2

Oligarchy – Commodification and Economic Democracy

1 Cornered and captured

Barely a quarter of a century ago, the Western economic model was seen by many elites around the world as hegemonic. After the end of the Cold War, capitalism had seemingly triumphed over communism and a global convergence towards liberal market democracy was apparently under way. Twenty-five years later the reality is one of monopoly markets in the West and state capitalism in the East.[1] The 2008 financial crash and the ensuing recession cast doubt on the capacity of liberal democracy to tame the forces of global capitalism. In response to the 'credit crunch', nation-states bailed out transnational banks by taking on their liabilities in a manner that relegates democracy yet further behind economic power. Elected government has less and less regard for the political ends of its citizens, while the long-term needs of national society are subordinated to the short-term interests of a worldwide financial oligarchy.[2] Instead of a democratic capitalism that distributes

34

power and wealth to all, we have a capitalist democracy that favours the fortunes of a few.

This chapter makes two arguments. First, liberal democracy is compatible and even complicit with the rise of a new oligarchy that concentrates wealth and power at the expense of the common good. Far from being a recent phenomenon, this has been a structural trend since the late nineteenth century, perhaps with the exception of the more embedded post-1945 market economy. But since the late 1970s the latter has given way to a disorganised, anarchic form of capitalism that revolves around the collusion between 'big government' and 'big business'. Subsidies from central government for corporations taking on debt, combined with support for the growth of global finance through light-touch regulation, have led to an economy that is captured by small yet powerful sectional interests that extract vast economic rents and exercise a cartel control of cronies.[3] For example, Amazon's dominance of online retail and other services has come about in part as a result of avoiding sales tax and benefiting from substantial public subsidies. In 2016, via the tax haven of Luxembourg, Amazon paid a mere £15 million in tax on EU-wide revenues worth £19.5 billion.

Western liberal market democracy, especially in its Anglo-Saxon variety, maintains the illusion of open, competitive markets that generate prosperity for the people while in reality enforcing monopoly and enriching a new oligarchic class of 'professionals' led by financiers. The result is an economy that is characterised by low growth, low productivity, low wages and low innovation in which maximising financial value leads to the destruction of productive capacity and the commodification of life. In turn, these forces undermine what the British Labour MP Rachel Reeves calls, in a ground-breaking pamphlet, 'the everyday economy, which is made up of the services, production, consumption and social goods that sustain people in their daily life at home and at work.'[4] Globalisation and the digital age are changing the context, but the fundamental task is to build a just economic and social settlement that combines new sources of prosperity with the protection of people in their families, communities and workplaces.

Second, a genuine alternative to oligarchy has to renew and strengthen the 'everyday economy' by building an economic democracy that Western countries have never had – apart from elements of Germany's social market before the introduction of the euro.[5] This will involve raising wages and sharing assets (not just redistributing income through state-rationalised welfare) as well as giving workers and employees more power in shaping their workplace. Some of the necessary reforms include new rights for workers in the 'gig economy' and new corporate governance arrangements – for example, workers' representatives on company boards – but also novel ways of bringing together government, employers' associations and trade unions in negotiated settlements. But none of these measures will be sufficient to redress the imbalance of power between the new *rentier* class of financiers and the rest. That is why existing anti-trust legislation has to be enforced, which means breaking up old industrial monopolies and new tech empires and penalising anti-competitive conduct such as predatory pricing. What is also required is action against capital concentration by mega-investors such as Warren Buffett and legislation to outlaw precarious and punishing jobs.[6] Another element of a more democratic economy is the strengthening or creation of new institutions such as regional banks and a People's Fund (financed partly by fining those businesses convicted of anti-competitive behaviour) with an annual dividend for all adult citizens.

The chapter will begin by outlining the chief characteristics of contemporary capitalism before charting the rise of monopoly and monopsony power over the past thirty years and then developing a series of transformative ideas that combine the break-up of oligarchic cartels with the building of an economic democracy based on open markets, a balance of interest within the firm and different forms of ownership.

2 The logic of contemporary capitalism

Contemporary capitalism is characterised by a concentration of wealth, a centralisation of power and a commodification of everyday existence. According to Oxfam, 82 per cent of the total wealth generated in 2017 was accrued by the top 1 per cent,[7] many of whom do not produce anything or own companies but instead make money out of money, largely by receiving dividends and interest payment as well as by speculating on the price movements of the stocks and shares they hold. In the USA, this amounts to capturing as much as 30 per cent of national income.[8] Power has also flown up – to the top management and large shareholders rather than to the wider workforce or small investors. Multi-million salaries, cash bonuses and golden handshakes have not only raised the ratio of income between top earner and average worker from about 45:1 to as much as 450:1

but also put in place a system of perverse incentives that reward both greed and corporate failure.

In the UK, the total pay of the chief executives of leading companies listed on the London stock exchange rose by 400 per cent in the period from 1998 to 2015, while most workers have seen their pay in real terms stagnate or decline since the 2008–9 financial crisis. A recent study by the Resolution Foundation think-tank suggests that real wages will not return to pre-crisis levels until 2025, leaving workers with an unprecedented seventeen-year pay squeeze that is exacerbated by cuts to public services.[9] The concentration of wealth is starving the economy of oxygen and perpetuates a model riven by inequalities of income and assets.

Unrestrained capitalism also reinforces an imbalance of power and interests in favour of the wealthy few. For example, large shareholders who know very little about the businesses in which they invest are often absentee owners, instructing their portfolio managers to speculate on stock-market movements or increasing market shares but taking no interest in how companies operate. For example, Warren Buffett's Berkshire Hathaway fund employs a mere twenty-five people who oversee more than sixty businesses and over half a trillion US dollars in assets. Together with Jeff Bezos of Amazon and Bill Gates of Microsoft, Buffett controls more wealth than the 160 million poorest Americans combined, and he paid just US$1.8 million in taxes in 2015 on his US$87 billion fortune – a mere 0.002 per cent tax rate.[10] Donald Trump's tax reform in 2017 earned Buffett US$29 billion. With multinationals paying disproportionately low taxes and workers suffering real wage decline and insecure jobs, a sense is spreading that it is one rule for the oligarchic few and another for everyone else.

Meanwhile, the commodification of everyday existence proceeds apace. The process of turning everything and everyone into a commodity goes far beyond the expansion of markets into previously non-monetised areas of life, of which the commercialisation of education and the sexualisation of children's clothing and entertainment are but two extreme examples. Commodification means stripping human beings and nature of any intrinsic worth and viewing them as exchangeable rather than irreplaceable. And commodifying knowledge involves the destruction of an inheritance and intergenerational innovation, while commodifying money is denying its symbolic significance as a token of exchange and trust. Commodification is based on subordinating society to the market in ways that reduce relationships to transactions, deplete the common resources of nature, and deny the sacred dimension of both human beings and the natural world.[11]

As markets and monetary transactions have expanded into society and our everyday lives, our natural environment, our inherited knowledge and our social relations have been captured by corporate capitalism and been turned into commodities. The logic that underpins the forces of concentration, centralisation and commodification is one which rewards the vice of greed and subverts both law and regulation based on sheer financial power.

As a result, the economy tends towards privatising profits, nationalising losses and socialising risks. By abusing their dominant market position (an issue to which I will return presently), large corporations raise prices and slash wages in a manner that increases their profit margins and boosts their stock market valuation while holding down their cost base. This has channelled a disproportionately large share of national income to capital owners at the expense of wage labourers. Real wages have stagnated for many, creeping up by barely 0.2 per cent per annum in the period 1973–2014 in the USA, even as in the same period productivity went up every year by 1.33 per cent. The recent rise in wages is little more than a snap-back.

Since a vast majority of companies have also spent less on capital investment, this paradox of declining labour and capital shares is explained by their monopoly power that has enabled them to produce higher mark-ups and keep greater profits.[12] Thanks to golden handshakes and other aspects of the dominant remuneration system, corporate losses are nationalised, in the sense of being deflected from top managers and shareholders to tax-payers, of which bank bailouts are emblematic. And the losses caused by the recession that followed the 2008–9 financial crash have been borne largely by those on low wages and dependent on local government services, who have been hit hardest by austerity.

Meanwhile, risk has shifted from the public and the private sector to individuals and families, who face new threats as part of globalisation – especially the systemic risk of financial contagion. Such systemic risks have long latency periods, so that their long-term consequences cannot be reliably determined and contained. A case in point is the build-up of debt as part of complex financial instruments such as derivative trading in the run-up to various financial crises. As a result of complexity and the opacity of chains of control, it is increasingly difficult to identify cause and effect, as with the vast financial Ponzi scheme of subprime mortgages whose implosion triggered the 2008 global credit crunch.[13]

In the final instance, contemporary capitalism is a system of destruction before being a system of production and exchange. It destroys intrinsic worth through the extraction of surplus value from labour and by fabricating consumer desire, which in turn are based on a double substitution: financial speculation replaces economic production and the material aggregation of personal preferences replaces the blending of material value with symbolic significance. Capitalism's indifference either to meaning or to natural variety renders it a destructive force – not an engine of creativity that values human labour and the imagination.

3 Monopoly

Binding together the privatisation of profit, the nationalisation of losses and the socialisation of systemic risk is the growth of monopoly and monopsony power. Both are forms of market domination that involve an abuse of power vis-à-vis consumers (monopoly) or vis-à-vis workers and suppliers (monopsony). Monopoly is as old a phenomenon as the market itself, but in recent times it has reached both a scale and an intensity that, compared with what took place in the first wave of modern economic globalisation in the second half of the nineteenth century, are unprecedented in terms of dominating the world economy rather than specific sectors or national economies. During this period of rapid industrialisation, the three monopolies that dominated the US economy were railways, sugar and oil: the US Steel Corporation controlled 67 per cent of the market, Standard Oil 87 per cent and the American Sugar Refinery Company 98 per cent. In 1911, President Theodore Roosevelt used anti-trust legislation to break up Standard Oil into thirty-four companies, at once ending its illegal monopoly power and making its founder, chairman and major shareholder John D. Rockefeller America's richest man, as the initial profits of the separate enterprises exceeded those of the single company. But since then the oil market has seen a vast consolidation around a few energy giants, including Chevron and ExxonMobil – itself the product of a merger – and the 'Big Six' energy companies dominating over 90 per cent of household energy in the UK.

For some time after the New Deal and the post-war settlement, monopoly power declined, but starting in the 1980s, and especially since the mid-1990s, over two-thirds of all economic sectors have seen a significant increase in the concentration of ownership and market control, from agriculture via manufacturing and industry to the service sector. Today liberal market economies are dominated by two types of monopoly power: old industrial corporations and new tech giants. Linking them is a novel oligarchy composed of financiers and a 'professional class' made up of managers, accountants, auditors and corporate lawyers, as well as regulators and politicians.

As the Democrat Senator Elizabeth Warren has remarked, the old industrial monopolies cut across numerous sectors:

> Four airlines control over 80 percent of domestic airline seats. Five health-insurance giants control over 80

percent of the health insurance market. Three drugstore chains have 99 percent of the industry's revenues. Four companies control over 85 percent of America's beef market. Two giants sell over 70 percent of all beer in America.[14]

And then there are the new tech giants of Alphabet/Google, Amazon, Apple, Facebook, Microsoft and the Chinese online empire Alibaba, each with a heavily dominant market position. For example, Facebook has over three-quarters of all mobile social networking traffic in the USA, with more than half of all American adults using it every day. Over 85 per cent of all new online advertising spending in the United States goes to Facebook and Google's parent company Alphabet, and this duopoly is currently responsible for referring over half of all online traffic to news websites. In total, Facebook has more than 2 billion users worldwide. Compared with the late nineteenth-century monopolies, today's tech giants wield much more power over the world economy on account of the data they control. Their market dominance enables them to charge more for online advertising and pay nothing for the behavioural data which they collect and which they then use in order to target individuals even more effectively than before. Data is the tech giants' life blood, and in their monopolistic hands it becomes a weapon with which the incumbents defeat potential market entrants while also manipulating consumer behaviour. This power has the potential to change markets from being open and public to being closed and private. Global capitalism supplants the everyday economy.

This concentration of market dominance among the

tech giants is not inevitable but in fact a relatively recent phenomenon. Less than ten years ago, when smartphones were still an emerging phenomenon, Google's market share for all internet searches was 66 per cent, not nearly 90 per cent as in 2017. Now that most search traffic has moved to smartphones, Google's market share for smartphone searches is a staggering 97 per cent. Taken together, the big five US tech giants are worth over US$3 trillion in market capitalisation, and at the end of 2016 their combined revenues were US$555 billion. Corporate consolidation is linked to the non-enforcement of anti-monopoly legislation in the face of waves of mergers and acquisitions fuelled by easy credit and an economy built on debt.

Both old and new monopolies share two fundamental traits. First, they have more than one producer, but the dominant players are in fact giant trading firms, designed to govern entire production systems from the producer all the way to the consumer, such as Walmart. Such trading firms secure easy credit (or use their own cash flows) in order to retail products that are often produced by suppliers at home or abroad.[15] Arbitrating between suppliers, workers and communities, they do not so much eliminate all competition as shift it from a horizontal to a vertical plane: from competition with other producers or service providers to competition with workers, suppliers, customers and the communities where businesses are located. In this vertical competition, trading firms seek ever greater price mark-ups, profits and market share rather than better quality at lower prices.

Second, monopolies tend to outsource production to large suppliers, suppressing competition along the supply chain and shifting production to low-wage, low-tax locations in ways that lead to corporate concentration at the top and the bottom of the sector. The car industry is a good example. A few large companies compete on brands made up of essentially the same parts, coupled with a small number of suppliers that provide the components. In the USA, for instance, C&A supplies cockpit assemblies, seats, flooring and door panels to more than 90 per cent of all car manufacturers, including American and Japanese makers. This process involves the vertical disintegration of the industrial firm whereby in-house part-making is spun off or shut down altogether in favour of outside suppliers.

Similarly, the main supermarket chains in the UK and the USA get their supplies from an increasingly small number of firms, such as Procter & Gamble, Unilever and Nestlé, that have swallowed up smaller suppliers. In each case, the consolidation of the supply base means that the entire sector is now dominated by giant trading firms at the top and cartels at the bottom that, taken together, form conglomerates 'too big to fail'. The growing interdependence along the chain means that failure somewhere can lead to failure everywhere, requiring taxpayer-funded bailouts – as with banks and car manufacturers in 2008–9. Corporate consolidation has created the conditions for 'cascading collapse',[16] which illustrates how profits are captured by a small elite, losses are borne by people and systemic risks are offloaded to society.

Monopoly power diminishes democracy in the market. First of all, it reduces competition in both price and quality, which contradicts standard economic theory that economies of scale provide efficiency gains and reward excellence. Take the airline industry, which since privatisation in the 1980s looks like a competitive sector with better service and lower airfares. But in reality the US and European market is dominated by a small number of airlines that control more than three-quarters of routes and seat capacity. In more than 90 of the leading 100 airports in the USA, a majority of all seats sold is managed by one or two companies. Through a combination of mergers and subsidiaries, airlines form part of vast conglomerates – for example, the International Airlines Group composed of British Airways and Iberia – that generate higher profits for their top management and large shareholders at the expense of staff and passengers.

Common ownership of airlines and their routes leads to airfares that are higher on average by between 3 and 7 per cent compared with separate ownership and more effective competition. Punishing hours and increasingly demanding working conditions for pilots and the on-board crew put pressure on workers. Crowded planes and more connections (which require ever faster airport turnaround times) make flying worse for ordinary customers, while the affluent can afford to pay extra for baggage, more legroom or priority boarding. Whereas in 1995 fees for 'extra services' represented just over 10 per cent of airlines' total revenue, today they amount to more than a quarter.

Market concentration in the banking sector has not just seen an unprecedented number of high-profile scandals, ranging from selling subprime mortgages to vulnerable customers via the manipulation of inter-bank lending rates to rogue trading. Banks are also routinely involved in low-level deception and fraud: signing up customers for fake accounts; imposing obscure banking charges; issuing unwanted insurance (such as the scandal around Payment Protection Insurance in the UK); falsifying records to increase mortgage charges; overcharging on foreign exchange; and outsourcing customer service to call centres with expensive telephone charges – all of which drive up the profits and reduce the quality of service offered by the cartel of commercial banks in the USA and the UK that control a large share of retail banking. Thus monopoly leads to higher prices and lower quality, which provides an income stream that attracts large investors. As Warren Buffett has openly said, '[t]he single most important decision in evaluating a business is pricing power. If you've got the power to raise prices without losing business to a competitor, you've got a very good business.'[17] Monopoly begets monopoly in an upward spiral that enriches the ruling oligarchy.

The second way in which monopolistic power destroys democracy in the market is through the extraction of economic rent, which can be conceptualised as excessive profits over and above the costs of production or service provision that enable incumbents to keep out potential market entrants by undercutting them. Even if incumbents are eventually replaced by new businesses (IBM or Nokia losing their previously dominant position), their dominance causes damage while it lasts and creates structures of dominance for new monopolists. The expansion of economic rent refutes the efficient market hypothesis because high prices and poor quality rip off consumers (as with airlines or banks) and entrench monopoly positions. This is particularly true for the internet-based tech giants that overcharge on advertising based on the behavioural data of individuals which they get for offering basic search, email or social media functions.

Their ability to extract rents is enhanced by (1) minimising taxation through locating in low- or no-tax jurisdictions; (2) price discrimination at a fine-grained individual level, combined with manipulating customers to become ever more addicted to online services; (3) infiltrating traditional industries based on data power (from retail to media); and (4) needing few employees and therefore spending a small fraction on labour while diverting the excess profits to owners, the top management and large shareholders. Taken together, these factors reinforce a shift in incomes from labour to capital and from unskilled to skilled labour, both of which underpin the economic inequalities that fuel the political insurgency led by figures such as Silvio Berlusconi and now Donald Trump. As David Dayen writes, 'This consolidation has vastly inflated corporate profits, damaged workers and consumers, stunted economic growth, and supercharged economic inequality.'[18]

Third, monopoly reduces innovation through a combination of mergers and exponentially growing costs of market entry. Seed investment and venture capital for start-up companies trying to challenge the internet giants have declined by more than 40 per cent since 2015. Any business attempting to take on Amazon, Facebook or Google is unlikely to secure investors' support and get the chance to compete even if they provide an innovative product or service, because the incumbents will either undercut them or buy them up. Jeff Bezos, the billionaire owner of Amazon, could not be clearer: 'When you are small, someone else that is bigger can always come along and take away what you have.'[19] In fact, Amazon is no ordinary monopolist. It is not a mere retailer but a producer of goods and services both online and in shops – as with the acquisition of WholeFoods and the building of a vast shipping and delivery operation with the ambition of replacing UPS and FedEx. Nor is it simply the dominant player in the markets in which it operates. Instead, Amazon is built to abolish existing markets and to put in place a new indispensable infrastructure on which online and offline commerce runs. As Stacy Mitchell writes in her in-depth analysis, Amazon's model

> is moving us away from a democratic political economy, in which commerce takes place in open markets governed by public rules, and toward a future in which the exchange of goods occurs in a private arena governed by Amazon. It's a setup that inevitably transfers wealth to the few – and with it, the power over such crucial questions as which books and ideas get published and promoted, who may ply a trade and on what terms, and whether given communities will succeed or fail.[20]

4 Monopsony

The other element driving contemporary capitalism is the power of monopsony, which allows corporate conglomerates to put pressure on suppliers and employees, keeping down prices and wages. In highly concentrated sectors – two-thirds of the entire economy – companies act like cartels as they control the prices and composition of their supplies as well as dictating employment conditions because workers have nowhere else to turn.

Indeed, both supply and labour markets are highly concentrated, and the lack of competition further empowers the giant trading companies.

This is a system that is rigged not just against suppliers but also and above all against workers. Wage growth has consistently been lower than productivity growth. Recent recoveries, especially since the recession of 2009, have seen real wages stagnate or grow at less than 1 per cent a year – compared with 4 per cent in the period from 1945 to 1973. Meanwhile the incomes of managers and supervisors have increased much more strongly, and their situation is greatly helped by Donald Trump's regressive tax cuts. Overall the labour share in the economy has declined for the past forty years and is near a record low, whereas profit margins are near record highs. The only way to sustain consumer spending is through a combination of drawing down savings and taking out debt: in the UK, household debt made up of personal loans and credit card borrowing is approaching £200 billion, while in the USA total household debt now stands at record levels of US$13 trillion.

The monopsony power of the monopolists is further increased by the decline in workers' bargaining power. Trade unions represent only 6.5 per cent of America's workforce in the private sector, and union contracts no longer link pay to inflation even as real costs of living consistently exceed the official inflation target of 2 per cent and outstrip pay rises. There is thus a link between corporate concentration, on the one hand, and rising income and asset inequality, on the other – with profits flowing upwards and precariousness engulfing the 'bottom' 80 per cent. As the Pew Center reported already in December 2015 (a year before Trump's election), the American middle class is declining at a faster rate than at any point since the 1930s.[21] This trend extends to Britain, where the government's own social mobility commission found in its last two annual 'state of the nation' reports that upward mobility has fallen to levels not seen since the 1920s.

Moreover, one of the routes from poverty and precariousness to middle-class stability is increasingly closed: setting up a business. The rate of business creation in Anglo-Saxon economies is down since the 2008–9 financial crisis, and fewer newly established enterprises survive and thrive over a period of five years or more. In the USA, the statistics paint a much worse picture, with a drop in new firms of almost 70 per cent since 1980 and a decline in small retailers by 85,000, which represents a 21 per cent fall.

Thus contemporary monopolies and cartels are not simply distorting market prices, consumer choice and the quality of products and services, from banking via water to food. They threaten to replace open, public markets with a closed oligarchy policed by a new moneyed aristocracy devoid of honour and virtue. This is a threat not simply to economic competition but also to democratic politics: by restricting or cutting off access to books or other sources of information and knowledge, Facebook and Google exercise control over public debate in ways that threaten not merely open markets but also free inquiry and free speech. For example, paid advertising offers the possibility of amplifying the virality of fake news. This suggests a feedback loop optimised for manipulation: make money on Google and then spend the proceeds on propaganda via Facebook – which will be discussed in chapter 3.

It is becoming ever more apparent that the economic logic of the Chicago School, with its focus on efficiency and free choice, has produced just the opposite: a *rentier* economy in which most consumers are denied real freedom of choice and are instead offered shoddy products and services in markets that are neither competitive nor open. As Mitchell concludes in her investigative analysis of Amazon, the platform monopoly of the tech giants 'can harm us as producers of value, not merely as consumers of it. And their control over our livelihoods and the fate of our communities is inherently political: it's a threat to liberty and democracy.'[22]

5 *The rise of the* rentier *economy*

A very brief history of how Western market economies got to this position is important in order to understand how monopoly capitalism operates and what can be done to build an economic democracy. The West's modern economy was founded upon the ambition of free and fair competition secured by the rule of law and regulation with a view to promoting producers – the farmer, the craftsman, the engineer and the entrepreneur. Western liberal democracies have had legislation for more than a century aimed at breaking up monopolies and curtailing the powers of those who break rather than produce things – encouraging innovation based on risk-taking, entrepreneurial freedom and protecting private property.

However, it was in the late nineteenth century that capitalism produced the first concentration of the modern market, which destroyed competition and led to the dominance by an oligarchic class made up of financiers, industrialists and captive politicians.[23] As already mentioned, three companies dominated oil, sugar and the railroads in the USA, prompting President Theodore Roosevelt to smash Standard Oil's monopoly in 1911 and leading Woodrow Wilson to declare on the presidential campaign trail in 1912 that 'The United States is never going to submit to monopoly. America is never going to choose thralldom instead of freedom.'[24] Faced with the threat of liberal *laissez-faire*, anti-trust legislation and the political will to enforce it were key to preserving liberty and promoting democratic practices in the economy.

During the interwar period, opposition to *laissez-faire* liberalism took the form of extreme statism – communist collectivism and fascist corporatism – that posed an existential threat to democratic politics and open markets. In response, the New Deal and the post-war settlement ushered in the dominance of the industrial corporation that was at the heart of modern attempts to build an economic democracy beyond liberal individualism and totalitarian statism. The industrial corporation is founded upon the vertical integration of the production process, which means producing all the necessary parts in-house because outside suppliers can manipulate prices and provide untrustworthy components. This was particularly the case for the car industry in the wake of the Fordist revolution and later for new sectors such as electronics, with IBM even producing its own screws.

Crucially, as Barry Lynn – executive director of the Open Market Institute – has argued, the industrial corporation provided not just employment and an income but also services that were social, cultural and intellectual in nature. This included pension and health-care provision as well as the transmission of inherited knowledge and skills and the adoption of new tech-nologies along the vertical chain of production.[25] Thus the industrial corporation was part of a wider model that shared both power and wealth by giving workers a role in governance arrangements and by being organised more like a corporate body than an individual writ large – an association of members that share in risks, rewards and resources. As part of the New Deal and the post-1945 settlement, legislators and regulators also sought to guarantee two conditions on which open, competi-tive markets depend: first, the ability of producers to be price makers rather than price takers and, second, equal access to services such as railway transport, which were in public hands. This created a level playing field among corporations and charted an alternative to the cowboy capitalism of the *laissez-faire* era and the central plan-ning of state communism.

Not that the industrial corporation was the pinnacle of economic democracy. There was still an imbalance of power between capital owners and wage labourers, and both had insufficient regard to the needs of nature and of civil society. Moreover, attempts to build a more democratic system of industrial relations failed in many Western liberal democracies, for example in the UK, where the government did not implement the recommen-dations of the 1977 Bullock Report, which promoted worker participation with a view to resolving increas-ingly acrimonious disputes, averting crippling strikes and giving employees not just a voice but some genuine power in their workplace. This Labour initiative was in response to the European Commission's proposals for a Europe-wide approach to worker representation. The then Labour prime minister, James Callaghan, was determined to overcome the conflictual industrial relations in Britain and tackle the low productivity that still besets Britain's economy today.

However, the dismantling of this corporate governance model over the past forty years has further diminished democratic arrangements within the firm as well as across the economy. Starting in the 1980s with the Reagan administration's reluctance to use anti-trust powers, industrial corporations mutated into trading firms that replaced vertical integration with horizontal specialisation – either dominating a whole sector or retreating in the name of efficiency. The policies of privatisation and deregulation put in place by Reagan and Thatcher unleashed a wave of mergers and acquisitions whereby companies such as General Electric concentrated their power in a few sectors where they had regulatory backing while avoiding competition with firms supported by mercantilist countries such as Japan and France. The overall strategy involved breaking up the diversified industrial conglomerates into highly specialised businesses with hegemonic market power. The foundations for corporate consolidation were laid and with it a new model of political economy focused on concentration, centralisation and commodification – a system of destruction rather than production.

In addition, successive US administrations abandoned the public management of trade in favour of a supranational system of governance (the General Agreement on Tariffs and Trade and then the World Trade Organization), combined with the rise of multinational corporations with no particular commitment to any industry or country. Robert Reich, President Clinton's secretary of labor, described the emerging global economy as follows: 'There will be no *national* products or technologies, no national corporations, no national industries. There will no longer be national economies. At least as we have come to understand that concept.'[26] The process of globalisation has always rested on the subordination of politics to the economy and of the nation-state to the unfettered global free market.

Combined with free-trade globalisation was the financialisation of the firm and the market economy in three stages: first of all, debt-financed mergers and acquisitions aimed at corporate concentration and the extraction of rents from suppliers and workers; second, rationalisation aimed at cutting the new mega-conglomerates back to size and paying off some of the debt, which leads to a sell-off of certain parts of the business, the elimination of products and thus a further consolidation of concentrated power; and, third, the expansion of the financial trading firm into new markets in pursuit of ever greater monopoly dominance based on rents. The takeover by the US-based company Kraft of the British business Cadbury exemplifies this process and the hollowing out of the social ethos, turning Cadbury from a force for social good founded upon Quaker ideals of restraint into an example of corporate greed that abandoned the commitment to fair trade and its contribution to community flourishing. In this manner, the socio-economic fabric woven in the wake of the New Deal and the postwar settlement has not just frayed at the margins but been torn apart.

Instead of challenging the new economic dogma of monopolisation, centre-left governments in the 1990s and 2000s took the policy of not enforcing anti-trust legislation to the next level. The Clinton administration not only repealed the Glass–Steagall Act that had separated retail from investment banking but also promoted mega-mergers across the US economy, as did New Labour under Tony Blair and Gordon Brown in the name of 'light-touch' regulation. After the 2008 financial crash some financial re-regulation did occur, including higher capital requirements, bail-ins and a greater isolation of retail bank deposits from the speculative activity of investment banking. But corporate consolidation has proceeded apace with new waves of mergers and acquisitions, as well as the fusion of giant corporations with state agencies.

An example is the company Carillion in the UK, which went bust under a debt burden of £2 billion even as it obviated market competition while its top managers enriched themselves on lavish government contracts funded by the taxpayer. As Will Hutton points out, Carillion 'was an ownerless company denuded of any purpose except seemingly to enrich its directors and keep its rootless multiple shareholders happy from one profit-reporting period to another. There was no mission to deliver, no drive for excellence, no pride in service. Workers were disposable notations on spreadsheets.'[27] An even greater degree of concentration applies to state-backed conglomerates from China, Russia and the Gulf States. In fact, authoritarian state capitalism is emerging as the most serious rival to capitalist market democracy since the rise of communism and fascism. Yet, at the same time, both have in common some structural features such as the concentration of power and the extraction of rents.

Monopolisation is both a source and a reflection of the

shift from the industrial corporation anchored in open markets to the financial firm supported by a new oligarchy. Indeed, the rise of the *rentier* economy has been driven by a new oligarchic class of professionals, chief of all financiers. Already in 1914, the commercial lawyer and future US Supreme Court justice Louis Brandeis observed that greed, a lack of accountability and poor oversight of the financial system allowed bankers to use 'other people's money' in order to manipulate markets to their own exclusive advantage – monopolising the profits while deflecting losses and spreading risk. Brandeis called this process the 'Money Trust'. Then, as now, economic power lies with financiers, who are middlemen between workers-savers and investors-producers and who 'bestride as masters of America's business world, so that practically no large enterprise can be undertaken successfully without their participation or approval.'[28]

This characterisation applies as much to global investment banks as it does to seemingly iconic investors such as Warren Buffett, a monopolist who supports fellow monopolists. As David Dayen writes in a profile of the Sage of Omaha, 'Buffett routinely takes advantage of opportunities unavailable to ordinary investors: The mega-bank Goldman Sachs created an internal "brain trust" solely to pitch deals to people like Buffett. "The kind of trades he does today no one else can do – you gotta be that big," explains David Nelson of Belpointe Asset Management.'[29]

The rise of the *rentier* economy confirms the argument that the institutions and procedures of liberal democracy are compatible with the power of oligarchy whereby both the USA and the UK have governments of, by and for corporate monopolies. These corporations subvert both open markets and democratic politics by exercising control over individuals and large sections of society. This convergence and collusion of 'big government' and 'big business' is not a new threat to popular democracy. Already in the 1830s, Tocqueville observed that the concentration of power in the hands of a corrupt oligarchy leaves the citizenry atomised and manipulated:

> [this union of power] accustoms citizens to set their own will habitually and completely aside; to submit, not only for once, or upon one point, but in every respect, and at all times. Not only, therefore, does this union of power subdue them compulsorily, but it affects their ordinary habits; it isolates them and then influences each separately.[30]

This means that tech giants not only enjoy monopoly dominance in the economy but also benefit from a total asymmetry of power vis-à-vis citizens, who are targeted individually and without any mediation (an issue to which chapter 3 returns). The techno-financial hegemony has hollowed out the public sphere and the polity. As the Italian economist Stefano Zamagni rightly remarks, 'a society in which democracy applies only to politics will never be fully democratic. A good society to live in will not force its members into uncomfortable dissociations: democratic as citizens and voters, undemocratic as workers and consumers.'[31]

6 Breaking up the 'empire of everything'

Enforcing existing anti-trust legislation is the first step in tackling monopoly power and creating the conditions for economic democracy. The principal problem is that Western politicians and regulators have tended to reduce the objective of anti-monopoly laws to a single, narrow goal of efficiency (as in the USA) or consumer choice (as in the EU), which is supposed to yield good-quality products and services at competitive prices. However, since the Reagan administration, the Federal Trade Commission's Bureau of Competition has rarely blocked mergers and acquisitions but, on the contrary, promoted aggressive corporate consolidation.[32] This process intensified in the wake of the 'light-touch' regulatory framework put in place by President Clinton and his team of advisers trained in the Chicago School of economics, with its focus on pursuing either more business efficiency or more consumer welfare.

By contrast, successive EU competition commissioners have intervened more forcefully, combining traditional concerns about mergers, abuse of market position and cartels with a new focus on anti-competitive state aid. The European Commission is known to impose substantial fines on repeat offenders such as Microsoft for abuses of competition policy, including the latter's refusal to supply its competitors with interoperability information and its tying behaviour in relation to streaming media players. However, Microsoft's market dominance remains largely undiminished.

In 2017 and 2018, the Commission fined Google €2.42 billion and €4.3 billion for abusing its dominant market position in relation to the operating system Android and its share of 95 to 98 per cent of internet searches in some EU countries. The charge is that Google stops manufacturers from selling smartphones running on rival operating systems and that it puts its own shopping results at the top of search lists and thereby disadvantages rival search sites. This decision is not limited to financial punishment but also requires Google to provide equal treatment to competitors. However, Google's response will either lead to higher consumer prices in the short term, which the Commission wants to avoid, or force rivals into a bidding process that is likely to eliminate them from the market altogether. Either way, Google's continued dominance underscores the limits of existing anti-trust policy, leaving authorities with little choice but to try to tax the profits of tech giants that engage in jurisdiction-hopping.

Therefore a new approach is needed in order to curb monopoly power and bring about open, competitive markets that offer genuine choice to consumers while at the same time balancing their interests with the interests of producers, workers and suppliers. Politicians such as the former US secretary of labor Robert Reich or the Democrat senator Elizabeth Warren have rightly argued that market dominance gives incumbents the opportunity to engage in predatory behaviour vis-à-vis consumers and citizens alike – abusing their power to extract excessive profits and influence legislators and regulators. In consequence, they have called for a revival of anti-trust action based on existing legislation that would block anti-competitive mergers, stop monopolistic conduct and prioritise protecting competition.[33]

While these measures would be a marked improvement on the prevailing policy for the past forty years, they are insufficient to tackle the root problem – the sheer size and reach of old industrial conglomerates and the new tech giants. This is a problem of economic theory as much as policy: the dominant Chicago School dogma of pursuing either more business efficiency or more consumer welfare needs to be abandoned in favour of promoting market diversity, a plurality of business models and supply-chain resilience. Therefore a more effective competition policy has to involve three radical reforms: (1) downsizing incumbents by breaking them up and enforcing interoperability with rivals; (2) introducing limits on ownership concentration; and (3) creating a People's Fund paying an annual dividend to all adult citizens, financed, for example, by fining those businesses that engage in predatory pricing and other anti-competitive abuses, so that the *rentier* economy is transformed into an economy that serves the many as well as the few.

Anti-monopoly policy has to begin by downsizing incumbents and breaking them up into smaller entities. This applies across the entire economy, from international airline groups via global banking conglomerates to the internet-based empires. Such an approach involves two elements. The first element is to reverse recent mergers and acquisitions, for example Facebook's purchase of WhatsApp and Instagram, Google's acquisition of Motorola and YouTube, or Amazon's takeover of WholeFoods. These and other acquisitions have allowed the mother monopoly to spread its tentacles by leveraging the original platform in ways that favour anti-competitive behaviour: through ownership of WhatsApp and Instagram, Facebook is in a position to use its data to undercut rival messaging and social image providers, just as Google's ownership of YouTube provides a rich data mine with end-to-end control – from email via web browsing to operating systems and advertising platforms such as Chrome or Android. Therefore anti-monopoly regulators should force monopolies to spin off newly acquired business lines, so that there is a structural separation of the core business from new activities. In the case of Facebook, this would entail separating its social media business from its messaging and its social image services and, in the case of Amazon, its e-commerce platform from its offline retail operation.

The other element is to connect the break-up of corporations into two or more businesses with an enforcement of interoperability in order to ensure real competition. For an e-commerce such as a downsized Amazon, this would mean becoming what Stacy Mitchell calls a 'common carrier, obligating it to offer all sellers access on equal terms, just as we did with the railroads.'[34] Google, instead of directing its users to its own products and services, should be forced to rely on its merit-based algorithms in order to power its local searches with rival search engines. This would not only spread advertising revenue more evenly and thereby enable smaller competitors to challenge Google's monopoly, but it would also likely produce a wave of innovation and start-up activity, as was the case when anti-trust cases were brought by the US federal authorities against AT&T, IBM and Microsoft. For Facebook, this means creating portable data that would allow users to export their full social graphs (a depiction of interconnected relationships in online social networks) to potential rivals. This would serve to diffuse information across the web and also break the proprietorial monopoly on data with which the tech giants manipulate consumers.

The second radical reform is to introduce limits on the concentration of ownership and control. Currently there is complicit collusion between the top management and large investors such as Warren Buffett, whose Berkshire

Hathaway fund holds substantial stakes in the dominant businesses within a single sector. For example, Berkshire Hathaway has invested more than US$1.2 billion in the four largest American airlines, enticed by rising profitability that is the direct result of multiple mega-mergers and common ownership by a small set of large institutional investors. As Martin Schmalz has argued, common ownership links between such investors have helped bring about increased airfares and reduced seat capacity, which add to the profitability of an already concentrated, oligopolistic sector. Common owners of multiple firms have a vested interest in reducing competition and further raising profitability.

Unsurprisingly, as Schmalz concludes, '[t]he airlines' stock prices took off when the news broke about Buffett's common ownership investment. Rather than competing to deliver better service at lower prices, all four airlines are soaring together.'[35] Legislation is therefore needed to restrict the size of holdings by single investors and to dilute common ownership of several companies in the same sector. Otherwise the oligarchy of the top 1 per cent will carry on making money out of money without creating value or encouraging competition and innovation.

The third radical reform is to create a People's Fund to distribute assets among citizens. Such a fund could be financed by the fines levied on companies that have been convicted of anti-competitive conduct and possibly by a share of the taxes paid by those businesses that have so far avoided them through jurisdiction-hopping or other evasive action. The revenue from fines and taxes would flow into a stock-accumulating sovereign wealth fund, from which adult citizens would receive a direct dividend based on annual gains – similar to the cheque that each Alaskan receives from the state's Permanent Fund. An alternative way of strengthening the distribution of common resources and enhancing accountability is the model of the Norwegian wealth fund, whereby the government, scrutinised by parliament, is directly involved in the corporate governance of the revenue generated by the country's energy wealth and acts as a countervailing force to the current tyranny of certain large institutional shareholders.

7 Building an economic democracy

Breaking up the monopolists is a necessary but insufficient condition to build an economic democracy. The current system is rigged against workers, and this requires a systemic transformation of the relation between capital and wage, starting with a greater share for labour in national income. Therefore the minimum wage needs to be enforced across all sectors, including the 'gig' economy, and it has to be gradually raised to the level of the 'living wage' and even the 'family wage' that allows a worker to feed herself and her dependants. The 'living wage' and 'family wage' will vary according to location and sector, but in general all wage growth should be linked to the increase in labour productivity.

After decades of weakening trade unions, legislators in liberal democracies need to step in and strengthen workers' ability to unionise and engage in collective bargaining, for example by confronting companies such as Walmart or Ryanair which, until recently, had a blanket ban on union membership. But trade unions themselves have to change fundamentally, away from the old command-and-control model of top-down diktats towards a greater balance of power between bosses and members. Trade unions also need to become much more representative of the workforce, with its growing share of women and young workers, and they have to enable workers to self-organise in sectors such as retail, social care and manual work – including cleaners, cooks, security guards and builders, whose numbers have grown significantly.

Establishing unions in these and other sectors requires a fundamental reorganisation of work, away from state centralism or free-market fundamentalism towards greater power for democratically self-governed intermediary institutions – from neighbourhoods via local government to professional associations. This could involve strengthening or creating the following institutions and arrangements:

1 a new national vocational fund that could bring together all estranged interests to coordinate training and through-life learning – including local government, businesses, trade unions, universities, colleges and training associations;
2 reformed employers' associations that oversee part-vocational entry qualifications in sectors such as medicine, law, banking and finance;
3 a renewed system of voluntary, free, guild-like institutions that help to instil ethos, uphold professional standards and help members in tangible ways, for example by assisting with the transfer of portable pensions and other entitlements when workers change employers;

4 creating or strengthening local chambers of commerce in countries such as the UK, France or
   Germany that bring together employers, trade
   unions and local government to negotiate wages and
   working conditions;

5 new royal colleges (or equivalent in countries other
   than Britain) for both old and new professions and
   vocations that are currently under-represented or
   not represented at all, including manual jobs and
   the services sector. Royal colleges and their char-
   ters can be vital institutions in fostering professional
   self-association and participation in the economic
   governance; they help to instil ethos and a commitment to excellence – and their remit could be
   expanded to co-determine (together with legislators
   and regulators) who has a licence to produce and
   trade and on what conditions such licences can be
   revoked (in case of serious criminal behaviour);

6 a move in secondary education away from rote
   learning and memorising facts in core subjects to
   creativity, autonomous thinking and developing
   the whole person, which could include vocational
   pathways in comprehensive schools that lead to
   vocational labour-market entry, for example part-
   apprenticeship, part-study at vocational colleges;

7 an expansion in the status, number and quality of
   both technical and vocational colleges, which could
   be co-funded by government, employers and trade
   unions.

Another element of defending the dignity of labour is
to oppose the fatalism of those who see automation as
inevitably destroying millions of jobs in the near future.

As the most in-depth study of the impact of automation conducted by the OECD in 2016 suggests, the march of the machines will not make half of the workforce redundant. Across developed economies, 'only' about 9 per cent of jobs are at a high risk of being replaced by computers or robots in the coming ten to twenty years.[36] Therefore the core argument of advocates of a universal basic income (UBI) that technological progress in the form of automation and artificial intelligence will eliminate the necessity of work for the many is flawed. Other reasons include the active discouragement of work, the intensification of inequality between those owning and controlling technology and everyone else, the sheer costs of financing a UBI that covers basic needs, and the lack of popularity (high taxes, insufficient income or the lack of justice, as the UBI breaks the link between contribution and reward). In short, the UBI combines technological determinism that denies people agency with a disregard for social obligation on which democracy depends for an elementary sense of cohesion.

Instead of uncritically accepting technological determinism, a new political economy should defend the value of work based on human creativity, social interaction and the need for interpersonal contact. The value of work lies in the dignity that comes with autonomy and the pride of a job well done. In an age of growing mental and physical health inequality, work provides a sense of purpose, meaning and social relationships on which people rely for their flourishing. In terms of policy, a defence of the labour interest includes creating new public trusts for the pooling of technological knowledge to replace the current patenting system in which, at present, the dominant patent model favours large private corporations over smaller, more innovative and social enterprises. It also involves fostering workplace innovation through continuous on-the-job learning and through-life training, better skills use, innovation around teamwork, and a culture of trust and cooperation rather than compliance.

A defence of the labour interest also involves strengthening the asset base of the economy, and every country's single greatest asset is its people. Just as GDP is a poor measure of a country's true wealth, so too does the notion of 'human capital' fail to capture the talents, vocations and capacity for innovation of individuals.[37] A new system of through-life education and training is needed that includes early-years intervention and programmes for disadvantaged households, less specialised secondary and tertiary education and, above all, a much greater provision of vocational education and training, as outlined above.

One avenue that has so far not been taken is to put in place hybrid pathways that fuse academic knowledge with vocational induction for professions that require both – such as law, medicine, engineering, banking and finance. Another route is to enable workers to have greater control over their own assets, for example portable pensions, which could be linked to a wider distribution of capital and ownership – whether of property and plant capacity or of financial investment in one's own or other firms – through employee ownership and other forms of participation.

At the same time, the pressure of technological progress on existing jobs means that those businesses that retain and retrain their workforce could be offered tax breaks and other incentives. There is a strong case for targeted state subsidies given to companies that keep workers on, invest in training and technological upgrades and contribute spare workers to public works programmes.

In addition to strengthening the power of workers, a new political economy needs to curb the power of financiers and the top management. The latter have siphoned off excessive profits, and it is now time for governments and parliaments to take action by increasing taxes on corporations that fail to reduce the growing gap between executive and worker pay. Moreover, the old remuneration system of rewarding greed and failure has to be replaced with genuine performance-related pay, with salary increases and bonuses linked to value creation over three to five years rather than financial valuation over one year: this means rewarding employment, innovation and production rather than rationalisation, 'efficiency gains' and destruction driven by stock-market fluctuations. As a reward for more social and ethical behaviour, companies that pay their workers the 'living' or 'family' wage and give them representation and power on the board, as well as curb executive remuneration, could be afforded preference in terms of public procurement and other government contracts.

More fundamentally, the primacy of short-term shareholder value needs to be replaced with a legal requirement that companies pursue primarily a clearly stated purpose of long-term economic and social benefit based on rewriting company law. This should not be taken as an attack on shareholders as a whole. Rather, it would necessarily involve a favouring of the longer-term over the short-term shareholder – whose holding today may sometimes be a matter of indifferent seconds. Longer-term investment would be made more attractive in terms of both higher and securer dividends and an increased measure of responsibility for the firm, which would tend to hold in check any executive exploitation. Equally, executives would be more empowered to guard against rogue shareholders who have not identified their own with the corporation's interest.[38]

As part of this cultural transformation, the divorce of the meaning of material market 'growth' from its root meanings of ethical flourishing should be called into question. If democracy could collectively imagine a shared scale of priority, it would also remove the scarcity-driven oscillation between relative emphasis on the respective imperatives of consumption and production, demand and supply. For this shared scale would infuse a greater sense of justice into transactions – prices, wages, shares – over and above prevailing conditions of exchange. We could then have some sense of a 'proper' price paid for a thing of a certain ethical as well as economic value; of a 'proper' wage or salary paid for a certain social task involving different degrees of talent, labour, scope, risk and need for the exercise of virtue; of 'proper' shares in a firm as between the weighed contributions of owners, managers, workers and suppliers. All these things need first and foremost to become habitual through the development of a new ethos. But at the same time they should at the limits of claimed infraction come within the purview of law and judicial debate. For once a company is required to have a social as well as an economic purpose (as all businesses do according to the 2006 UK Companies Act and similar legislation elsewhere), then all contractual exchanges should by

71

law be equitable as to substantive content as well as to formal consent.

In conclusion: the overarching aim of these proposals is to tackle the concentration of wealth that is ingrained in the logic of liberal capitalism and the centralisation of power that underpins it. Instead of a corrupt oligarchy that entrenches the rule of the oligarchic class, the proposed alternative is about a more virtuous economic democracy that serves the many and the few.

3

Demagogy – Sophistry and the Politics of Truth

1 Liberal democracy's descent into demagogy

Liberal democracy faces the permanent threat of illiberal, demagogic forces that challenge individual liberties paradoxically in the name of free speech – as in the case of far-right racist groups, the revolutionary left or religious fundamentalists. However, the expansion of liberal democracy can itself be a catalyst for demagogy, as the use of 'corporate populism' by liberal elites tends to provoke an anti-liberal backlash. In response to the arrogance of the liberal expert class and its selective use of evidence that ignores inconvenient truths, Western democracies witness the periodic emergence of insurgent movements, as with Silvio Berlusconi and now Donald Trump, that are built on conspiracy theories, misinformation disguised as 'alternative facts' and naked appeals to both bigotry and race. In different ways, and without implying moral equivalence, both elitism and insurgency resort to demagogic manipulation of people by appealing either to technocratic facts or to sensationalist emotions.

73

Bound up with this is the question of truth and the liberal accusation that insurgents promote a politics of 'post-truth'. But one problem with contemporary liberalism is that it has itself a reductive and impoverished conception of what is true. Liberals do one of two things: either they reduce truth to the evidence of positivist science and instrumental rationality and ban substantive truths that go against these standards from the court of public debate, or else they deny any universal truth in the name of incommensurable values. Instead of pursuing the truth, liberalism institutes ground rules of fairness (as in the legalistic liberalism of John Rawls or Ronald Dworkin) or clings to some notion of discursive reason (as in the cosmopolitan liberalism of Jürgen Habermas).[1] Either way, both reject any metaphysical conception of what is true or good in favour of procedure. Nothing is allowed to make any substantive or critical contribution to public political discussion that could undermine the primacy of formal, procedural reason. But the slogan 'reason alone' leads to the dissolution of rationality – to the conclusion that only will and power have any reality. At a time when both elites and insurgents not only flout the rules but also violate the informal norms of democratic debate, such as respect for political opponents or a plural search for the common good, it is precisely will and power that hold sway.

The argument in this chapter focuses on ethos and truth. Even if truth can never be fully known and will always be contested, politics without some measure of substantive truth is sophistry, as ancient Greco-Roman philosophers such as Plato, Aristotle and Cicero warned. Today we are seeing democracy's descent into demagogy in large part because both liberals and insurgents are concerned more with will and power than with the pursuit of truth in a spirit of debate that reflects plural views and interests. Therefore the proposed alternative begins with a transformation of the media and political discourse that is generally neglected by liberal democracy. The first element is to enforce media plurality by breaking up the large empires and by treating the tech platform as media corporations powered by their monopoly over online advertising. Such a transformation should involve the unbundling of services in order to inject more competition into the market and to dismantle the echo chambers that are dominating democratic debate.

The second element is to foster a novel ethos that promotes a plural search for truth rather than mere opinion, which tends to descend into sophistry. Ethos in public discourse involves not just more evidence than liberal technocracy or anti-liberal conspiracy but also better judgement and a sense of the common good. The latter encompasses mutual recognition of everyone's talents, vocations and possible contribution to society, as well as the natural tendency of human beings towards 'common decency' (George Orwell) and honourable performance – proper pride in a job well done. In short, one argument this chapter develops is that a vibrant democracy requires some shared informal norms, including robust debate, viewing your opponent as a legitimate opponent instead of an enemy, and a joint concern for mutual flourishing rather than merely personal advancement at the expense of others.

2 Liberalism's demagogic drift

Liberal democracy rests on the assumption that only liberalism can free us from the tyranny of the Good – the imposition of a single conception of goodness, truth and beauty. The liberal tradition, with its securing of individual rights based on the rule of law, has certainly provided more freedom from oppression and persecution as well as greater opportunities for women and minorities – even though discrimination and inequalities persist. Yet, at the same time, increasing equality before the law has coincided with growing inequality of status and wealth, which has paved the way for the centralisation of power and the concentration of assets in the hands of an oligarchic few, with a resulting diminution of the scope for the shared quest of commonly accepted goals. This quest is what the ancients and their modern disciples called positive freedom – the liberty to pursue a joint purpose.[2]

A key characteristic of contemporary liberalism concerns the replacing of substantive notions of the good with a form of freedom that slides into empty free choice. Liberty is now 'negative' – the absence of constraints on individual desire apart from the law and private conscience.[3] Legal permissions given to some are seen by others as arbitrary refusals. Without any sense of the good we share in common with others, liberal freedom cannot decide between what should be allowed and encouraged and what should not. When rival rights and freedoms collide, power decides, and it is the liberal state that ends up ruling over individuals – of which Hobbes's Leviathan is the first and hitherto unrivalled expression. Contemporary liberalism's equating of liberty with the freedom to choose is manipulative because no positive forms of freedom aimed at shared ends are permissible within a liberal settlement that defines the horizon for economic or political decisions. Zygmunt Bauman puts this well: liberals promise ever greater freedom of choice, but 'the conditions under which choices are made are not themselves a matter of choice.'[4] For liberals today, there is no alternative to liberal liberty.

The liberal indifference to substantive values such as the good life also involves a tendency to exploit fear and manipulate opinion. Liberalism claims to offer security by guarding us against all enemies of freedom, but it fails to tolerate those who challenge its governing assumptions, above all the primacy of the individual over groups or communities. In fact, for liberals, human beings are rational, self-owning individuals who owe nothing to society – a philosophy of possessive individualism whose roots go back to Hobbes and Locke in the seventeenth century.[5] Liberalism also separates fact from value and privileges supposedly enlightened elites over the common sense of the people. That is why liberal democracy is caught between the pseudo-scientific truth of technocrats and the emotive 'post-truth' of insurgents. For liberals, everything – apart from the dangers of liberalism – can be debated publicly, including the personal, private sphere. Those who question the liberal consensus are branded anti-liberal and their views are dismissed as illegitimate. Liberalism's claim to tolerance flips over into intolerant illiberalism.

Liberalism's indifference to the good unravels into human self-domination by its own productions and into a further indifference to truth that transcends objective rationality and subjective emotion. A concern with truth reveals more complex principles about our humanity, such as the interplay of vice and virtue, than extremes such as egoism or altruism. It also discloses deeper insights about the natural world, which is neither purely in flux nor essentially static. An indifference to questions of substantive truth turns liberalism into a form of sophistry – the dominance of subjective opinion at the service of power over objective truth at the service of the common good. For the ancient Greek sophists, for example the historian Thucydides, reality is divided between nature and law, with truth sacrificed on the altar of a never-ceasing oscillation between natural chaos and the artificial imposition of order. The same nature/culture dualism is revived by neo-sophistic tendencies in modernity, most of all Hobbes, who posited an irreconcilable divide between anarchy in the 'state of nature' and the artifice of the social contract.[6] Truth is never fully revealed or known by finite human beings, but, for liberals, truth is purely subjective – a cultural construction of the mind rather than a reflection of natural reality.

For much of the modern age, liberals tended to assume that nature and culture have nothing to do with each other, because nature is inherently meaningless and mostly inciting of blind passions, while culture rests on law and is entirely artificial and arbitrary.[7] This ensures that individual emotions are little more than conscious manifestations of a blind will-to-power that needs to be regulated by humanly invented law. In turn, the liberal conception of the nature/culture divide is founded upon a deep anthropological pessimism according to which human beings are selfish, greedy, distrustful of others and prone to violence.[8] Once again liberalism owes an enduring intellectual debt to Hobbes and Locke, who believed in a violent 'state of nature' from which only the social contract can save us – a notion shared by Kant and Rousseau. Since our humanity is so clearly depraved and deprived of goodness, liberalism comes down firmly on the side of culture in the sense of human artifice and the idea that ultimately all is socially constructed, which implies that all can be deconstructed and undone, including our nature and the natural world. This subordination of truth to human self-determination and the will-to-power lies behind the slide of liberalism into sophistry and liberal democracy's demagogic *dérive*.

The liberal practice of demagogy ends up undermining the principles of liberality on which liberalism rests, including free inquiry, free speech and tolerance – a process of self-erosion in which the liberal tradition mutates into the hyper-liberal creed, as I argued in the introduction. Liberal politics thereby produces the very threats from which it supposedly protects us – ideological tyranny and the closing-down of argument. University 'safe spaces' and echo chambers on social media are indicative of a culture that leaves young people unprepared to deal with views other than their own. Group-think and subtle forms of censorship replace reflection and vigorous debate. Dissent is seen as propagating discrimination, and the accusation of 'hate speech' has itself become a form of hate speech as it is being deployed to silence critics, as the no-platforming of feminists such as Germaine Greer by transgender activists shows. The result is a political culture that is increasingly narcissistic and unable to build broad alliances. Paradoxically, liberalism brings about the kind of intolerant illiberalism that it ascribes to all non-liberal positions.

The other element of contemporary liberalism is social egalitarianism and individualised identity politics. From the 1960s onwards, liberals celebrated the diversity of difference at the expense of civic ties that bind people together beyond the divides of class, colour, creed, age, wealth or gender. The loss of a shared national identity and mutual obligations undermined social cohesion and civic patriotism. As Mark Lilla has argued, 'in recent years American liberalism has slipped into a kind of moral panic about racial, gender and sexual identity that has distorted liberalism's message and prevented it from becoming a unifying force capable of governing.'[9]

Already in the 1970s, Christopher Lasch argued that liberalism was becoming increasingly associated with a move away from the family and mutual obligation towards a culture of narcissistic self-absorption and political retreat into the private sphere of subjective self-expression.[10] The 1980s, far from witnessing a revival of civic spirit, saw the rise of yuppie greed and self-gratification whose economic excesses were mirrored in their social transgressions. A bunch of weed-smoking hippies morphed progressively into a generation of middle-aged, cocaine-fuelled financial speculators, as vividly depicted in the film *The Wolf of Wall Street* based on the memoirs by the former stockbroker Jordan Belfort, who pleaded guilty to charges of securities fraud and money-laundering. The rise of global finance, driven by legislative and regulatory incentives to greed, has divided society and subordinated national interest to multinational corporations. Our age of anger is a response to the economic and cultural excesses.

Today many leading liberals patronise or simply ignore those who neither support economic-cultural liberalism nor benefit from its effects. Free global trade, mass immigration and cosmopolitan multiculturalism have brought gains to the professional class but also losses to working-class communities, which experience economic and cultural insecurity. Instead of building bridges between estranged interests and identities, individualised identity liberalism entrenches a sectarian, minority politics at a time of polarisation. The commentator Ross Douthat goes further than Lilla, to suggest that

> people have a desire for solidarity that cosmopolitanism does not satisfy, immaterial interests that redistribution cannot meet, a yearning for the sacred that secularism cannot answer . . . . A deeper vision than mere liberalism is still required – something like 'for God and home and country,' as reactionary as that phrase may sound. It *is* reactionary, but then it is precisely older, foundational things that today's liberalism has lost. Until it finds them again, it will face tribalism within its coalition and Trumpism from without, and it will struggle to tame either.[11]

3 The demagogy of identity politics

It is not just contemporary liberalism that is being repudiated. The political traditions that were dominant for much of the nineteenth and twentieth centuries are dissolving.[12] In the USA and Britain, the Conservatives' reputation for being competent and reliable lies in tatters. Their economic model of free-market capitalism is broken. Continental European social democrats and socialists have abandoned their traditional working-class supporters in favour of a largely urban metropolitan electorate. Their social model of multiculturalism divides society. And everywhere the obsession with the identity politics of minority groups excludes a majority from the political mainstream.

Identity politics is about a shift from a sense of sacrificial contribution to the common life based on the struggles of representative democracy and collective agency to a culture of victimhood, a movement politics of protest and narcissistic online echo chambers of private preference. It marks the triumph of the 1960s motto that 'the personal is the political'. None of the ideologies has much to say about what people share as citizens or what binds them together as nations and cultures. Both left and right have embraced variants of identity politics, which has left them without a broad moral outlook. First the New Left from the mid-1960s onwards took socialism in a doctrinaire direction that was abstract and soulless. It equated the purpose of the left not so much with the struggle for greater economic justice as primarily with cultural liberation. Henceforth socialists preferred progress to tradition, identity to class, and free choice to common purpose. Then the New Right combined a libertarian economics with a corporate capture of the state. This had the effect of aligning conservatism with borderless capitalism and with individual freedom devoid of mutual obligation. An unholy alliance of fundamentalist faith with an aggressive consumer culture trumped the historic commitment to citizenship. Across the West the political contest descended into the culture wars, fuelling the flames of tribalism and polarisation on which the liberal elites and the anti-liberal insurgents seem to be thriving.

The radical right and hard left have stepped into this void. The alt-right around Donald Trump and anti-liberal strongmen across the globe want protectionist borders to have more 'neoliberalism in one country'. The Tory arch-Brexiteers have similar plans for a low-regulation, low-tax economy boosted by free-trade deals with the other countries of Anglo-Saxondom. So far, the policies of 'America first' and 'take back control' serve oligarchic interests with more than an undertone of nationalism.[13] Meanwhile, the hard left around Jeremy Corbyn, Spain's Podemos and Greece's Syriza pursues a utopia of 'socialism in one country', fusing twentieth-century-style economic interventionism with twenty-first-century digital platforms. It offers a future for the new, networked generation of globally mobile cosmopolitans. The rest will subsist on a universal basic income funded by taxing tech companies. Automation and artificial intelligence promise to create a post-capitalist economy without work or workers.[14]

For all their differences over open borders and multiculturalism, the radical right and the hard left share a certain anti-liberal outlook that is deeply demagogic. First, both clamour for more central state intervention to shield citizens from the effects of globalisation. They combine protectionism with welfare to restore national sovereignty. Second, both invoke the supposed will of 'the People' in ways that are reminiscent of 1930s authoritarianism. This poisonous propaganda ignores people as they are in their families, localities and workplaces. Third, both demonise their political opponents while rejecting any criticism of their leader as an act of sacrilege and blasphemy. In a divided era when politics needs common ground more than ever, the extremes preach a puritanism that is even more self-righteous than hyper-liberal identity politics.

Finally, both after all still view human beings in a fundamentally liberal fashion mainly as bearers of individual rights and carriers of economic laws, which reflects a preference for technological forces over human creativity and real political agency. This deterministic worldview is of a piece with top-down authoritarian control. Power is exercised by the leadership and patrolled by a Praetorian guard – Breitbart at the service of Trump and the vanguard of Momentum around Corbyn. Democracy is good as long as dissent is directed at the enemy. Like the sophists in antiquity, the political insurgents of today view truth as an exchangeable commodity in the marketplace of identity.

The descent into demagogy is perhaps nowhere more visible than in the sham debate about 'post-truth'. The (previously) ruling elites are shocked by the sheer transgressive nature of the political insurgency that is sweeping Western liberal democracies. They feign moral outrage when candidates such as Trump use social media to wage a demotic campaign, denouncing 'fake news' while deploying 'alternative facts' and racial slurs. Like rabbits in headlights, liberals and conservatives have not come to terms with mass movements against the establishment in both main parties and the traditional media. As John Gray puts it, '[i]n his core constituencies, efforts by mainstream media to demonstrate his mendacity have only reinforced the image Trump had fashioned for himself – that of being a truth-telling outsider besieged by Washington power elites determined to destroy him.'[15] Both sides accuse each other of hiding the truth, thereby fuelling conspiracy theories, which are based on the assumption that the truth is so self-evident that it must be concealed.

The fundamental problem is that many established journalists and politicians have been economical with the truth, focusing on those facts that fit into their liberal or conservative worldview and regurgitating the same progressive narrative about how globalisation, free trade and immigration benefit the people – with the 'culture wars' being the exception that proves the rule of this bipartisan consensus. The political mainstream, together with the support of media barons, embraced a utilitarian liberalism according to which the economic benefits of this consensus outweigh the costs. This is held up as an incontrovertible truth that only the racists, bigots and uneducated would deny, even though the evidence suggests that the working class and increasingly the middle class lose out due to pressures on wages, public services and settled ways of life.[16]

Another problem is the culture of victimhood around the current political insurgency. Just as the insurgents paint themselves as the target of establishment attacks and vilification, so too the ruling elites use catch-all terms such as 'post-truth' to dismiss the popular movements that propelled insurgents to power. Like 'populism' and 'authoritarianism', 'post-truth' is bandied about as something irrational and new when in reality demagogy based on information technology has always been part of politics. Political lies and spin are as old as the art of rhetoric and persuasion – hence Plato's public philosophy in response to the sophists.

According to the journalist Matthew d'Ancona, 'What is new is not the mendacity of politicians, but the public's response to it. Outrage gives way to indifference and, finally, to collusion.'[17] But is that a true depiction? Is it not rather the case that people trust their politicians less precisely because they play fast and loose with the truth? Characterising our times is people's realisation that lying is the new norm, not the exception, and that this applies to illiberal undemocratic liberalism perhaps as much as to anti-liberal insurgencies or elective autocracies which sport the trappings of democracy. What is true is now a matter of blind belief divorced from reason and grounded in subjective emotion.

Truth is little more than someone's personal preference and opinion, which by definition is just as valid as anyone else's. The reduction of moral and political judgement to emotivism has a long history in Enlightenment thinking, where culture, class and ideology have been conceptualised as sources of value and truth.[18] The post-modern obsession with the social construction of reality based on unmediated emotion is but an intensification of modern Enlightenment. In politics, this takes the form of what Harry Frankfurt calls 'bullshit', by which he means the sophistic subordination of truth to rhetoric as opposed to the Platonic, Aristotelian or Ciceronian conception of rhetoric at the service of truth.[19] It is not the case that all truth is discarded; rather, it is that truth is equated with a naked appeal to emotions of fear and intimidation.

The point that Frankfurt makes is that 'bullshit' pervades politics. Just as the insurgency practises the dark arts of demagogy, so too the establishment manipulates

public opinion – of which 'Project Fear' during the referendum campaign on Britain's EU membership is perhaps
the most egregious example in recent history. Both the
insurgents and the ruling elites they are trying to dislodge
converge around a politics of sophistry that combines a
relativist conception of truth with an absolutist moralism: neither group denies the truth outright, but they
equate it with subjective sensation and therefore view it
as absolute, since all emotions are now held to be equally
valid. Thus, at the hands of both the mainstream and
the alternative media, truth becomes light on informed
judgement and heavy on hysterical emotion. Critical
scrutiny gives way to panic and mutual demonisation,
which make reasonable debate increasingly impossible.

Whereas opponents used to be seen as legitimate
adversaries, now people on opposing sides view each
other as enemies, and each tries to manipulate the public
with rival brands of demagogic politics. The middle
ground is being abandoned in favour of a doubling
down on abstract liberal cosmopolitanism or a retreat
to nationalism and even atavistic ethnocentrism. Hyper-
liberalism and 'peak populism' fuel each other and look
set to endure. Faced with these extremes that are mirror
images of each other, the real alternative is between a
politics of substantive, commonly shared objective truth
and a politics of sophistry, subjective emotion and individualised identity.

4 Social media manipulation

One key thing that has changed compared with earlier eras is how the internet and social media have

transformed information, knowledge and public debate, with new communications and political technologies giving deception and demagogy added potency because the absence of gatekeepers eliminates accuracy, accountability and the differential status between lies and truth. As James Ball has shown, the economics of the web is undermining investigative journalism and accurate reporting in favour of sensationalism, hyperbole and hysteria.[20] Once more, it is the oligarchy in charge of online information and social media that drives democracy's descent into demagogy.

Even worse for democracy than the concentration of corporate control are the nature and level of social control exercised by the tech giants, notably social media. Facebook's platform, with its 2 billion users, instead of binding people together and creating a global community, reinforces cultural tribalism and political polarisation by encouraging users to link up with others who agree with them. The combination of filter bubbles with echo chambers fragments the public sphere and undermines the bonds of citizenship and common culture. In turn, a more fragmented polity is further divided by manipulated opinion masquerading as official facts or 'alternative facts' – whether in the mainstream media or in the insurgent media. Politics has always been ideological and partisan, but now it is being privatised, and debate increasingly takes place in silos where deception and demagogy cannot be challenged so effectively.

The tech giants manipulate the public in other ways too. One way is by stripping content providers of their creation and thereby eliminating competition from alternative mechanisms of provision, which has squeezed the creative and media industries and thereby undermines the diversity of both products and services because it shuts down innovation and new human creativity. For example, the music industry has gone from being worth US$20 billion in 1999 to US$7 billion in 2014, depriving many musicians of their income and giving *de facto* control to YouTube, where music is available essentially for free.[21] This goes against plurality and a balance of interests that are vital for democracy. The same applies to the tendency of internet corporations and chain stores to turn consumers into co-workers and exploit their free labour. As Jonathan Taplin reports, people on Facebook spent a combined 39,757 years on the site every day of 2014, when it had 1.2 billion users, producing content that is monetised by the corporation based on 'almost fifteen million years of free labour per year'.[22] This adds to the extraction of economic rent and further reinforces corporate control over people. The mechanism of controlling citizens as consumers and as users of social media is through the capture and sale of attention[23] – an influence over people's time and minds that far exceeds the power of government.

Indeed, tech platforms such as Facebook and Google are giant advertising companies that operate simultaneously like a media conglomerate and a political machine. In 2017, Facebook's annual advertising revenue was US$40 billion and Google's US$95 billion, while ad revenue for newspapers in the USA has fallen to under US$20 billion. This has led to huge job cuts in terms of reporters on the streets, reducing reliable sources of trustworthy journalism and strengthening the gatekeeper status of tech platforms – with over 90 per cent of Americans getting their news online and an overwhelming majority of them through the tech duopoly of Facebook and Google. The failure to enact anti-trust legislation means that they are free to strip advertising revenue from publishers and direct readers to and from publications at will.

Moreover, Facebook's shift from expanding the number of users to monetising their use involves new forms of manipulative advertising. Facebook's founder and CEO Mark Zuckerberg, when launching Facebook Ads, declared that 'Nothing *influences* people more than a recommendation from a trusted friend. A trusted referral is the Holy Grail of advertising.'[24] Internet-based corporations have unprecedented tools for micro-targeting consumers and voters – with the boundaries between the two becoming increasingly blurred. John Lanchester rightly concludes that 'What this means is that even more than it is in the advertising business, Facebook is in the surveillance business. Facebook, in fact, is the biggest surveillance-based enterprise in the history of mankind. It knows far, far more about you than the most intrusive government has ever known about its citizens.'[25]

Based on this knowledge, the tech platforms do not simply provide a space for consumption or debate but actively channel products and news to their users and are thereby engaged in demagogic action. What people see on their news feeds or their search results is not limited to the interests and recommendations of friends but encompasses content that is determined by commercial interests and driven through algorithms known only to the monopolists. This lack of transparency and accountability exacerbates the growing imbalance of power that is incompatible with a genuine representative government.

But the problem does not lie exclusively with those in charge of the tech giants or the legislators and regulators who fail to act on monopoly power. The behaviour of us as users is also problematic. The platforms provide new possibilities that encourage some of the lowest instincts characterising our human nature. We behave accordingly in ways that suggest a self-fulfilling prophecy – an expectation of anthropological pessimism (we're selfish, greedy and deceptive) that is confirmed by our individual and collective actions. There are two elements to this. First, many social media users poison public debate by trading on the internet's key currency – attention – through outrage and endless provocation. Not to respond is to be absent from the 'conversation' and to risk looking complicit. To respond is to appear to be lending legitimacy to the other side in the 'debate' and to amplify the original message, of which Donald Trump's tweets are the clearest example. There is also an endless feedback loop with online trolls who hide behind a veil of anonymity to spread poisonous propaganda with viral speed. By contrast, in real life and in relationships with flesh-and-blood people, an overwhelming majority of human beings do not behave in such craven ways.

Second, the growing disconnection between traditional media led by editors and journalists, on the one hand, and the alternative user-generated media, on the other, means that public debate is taking place in parallel echo chambers that are increasingly privatised while also abolishing privacy. It is driven not by what people need or what is good for them but by what gets their attention, which is based partly on lies and partly on Frankfurt's notion of 'bullshit'.[26] That people lie to themselves and to others is not new, but what is new is the sinister manipulation by social media platforms to turn lies into a blatant disregard for the truth and thereby to encourage 'bullshit'. Facebook's motto used to be 'make the world more open and connected', when it did just the opposite by linking together the like-minded who are less likely to care about lies. And when Zuckerberg announced the new motto ('a social infra-structure to build a global community') and promised to tackle fraudulent content, his Facebook post ran next to 'fake news'. For as long as social media is driven by the monetisation of its user base, it will promote atten-tion-seeking content and behaviour that undermines real relationships, thus further weakening the social cohesion, trust and cooperation on which democracy depends.

And then there is the collusion of social media cor-porations with data companies that help run election campaigns – as exemplified by the case of Facebook allegedly selling personal data to Cambridge Analytica for its work on the Trump campaign. As Jamie Bartlett has argued, the move towards data-driven elections changes the nature of politics. Voters are seen as data points that are targeted by machine-generated ads tai-lored to narrow personal preference. In this process, politics is not about argument and vision but instead about psycho-graphics and nudges. In turn, this favours those not just with money but also with access to personal data rather than those with good ideas and arguments. Linked to this is the sheer atomisation of the public political realm as a result of micro-targeting and the refusal of open debate in the name of individu-alised identity. Without overarching themes, the public commons fragments into a collage of private messages.

Instead of a broad political contest anchored around rival narratives, we have culture wars, 'wedge' issues and a retail policy offer for the citizen *qua* consumer. Bartlett concludes that,

> In the long run, the constant a/b testing and targeting might even encourage a different type of politician. If politics drifts into a behavioural science of triggers and emotional nudges, it's reasonable to assume this would most benefit candidates with the least consistent principles, the ones who make the flexible campaign promises. Perhaps the politicians of the future will be those with the fewest ideas and greatest talent for vagueness, because that leaves maximum scope for algorithm-based targeted messaging. What's really terrifying about all this is not how outrageous it is, but how normal it has already become.[27]

5 Power and ethos

Liberal democracy's descent into demagogy reveals both an excess of power and a lack of ethos. The former concerns the concentration of influence in the hands of old elites and new classes, which requires a break-up of monopolies, as outlined in chapter 2. This applies both to the mainstream and to the alternative media – Rupert Murdoch's TV and newspaper media empire as much as the tech giants. For example, the sheer size and control of ownership leads to an absence of competition: YouTube, with its 1.5 billion users, owned by Google's parent company Alphabet, is the only serious rival to the mother monopoly of Facebook, with its 2 billion users and its daughter companies WhatsApp, Messenger and Instagram, with their 1.2 billion, 1.2 billion and 700 million users respectively. This corporate control also has a 'force multiplier' effect, whereby bad practice crowds out good practice – attention-seeking narcissism that fuels individualised identity politics rather than a shared quest for commonly shared purposes such as human flourishing. Part of the response to this problem is to unbundle various services, separating social media businesses from messaging and social image services.

Another imperative is to subject the duopoly of Facebook and Google to the rules and regulations of media corporations. Far from simply being platforms that distribute news, they are operations that manufacture and channel (mis)information. As such, they should have to abide by media law in whatever jurisdiction they are active – whether national (USA and UK) or supranational (EU). This is all the more urgent since tech platforms such as Facebook have denied colluding with data companies such as Cambridge Analytica to use personal data without the consent of users in order to build detailed political profiles of around 30 million US voters who received targeted news on their social media feeds, which – if true – would be in violation of Facebook's own rules.

The latter problem of a lack of ethos concerns the vital issue of purpose and questions of truth. In the long run, an ethos of truth and truthfulness is more realistic than mere realism.[28] That is because ethos is about the sustaining of high quality and a commitment to recognise and advance the common good, however fragile, without which the members of a shared polity cannot flourish. And, without such a commitment, a vibrant democracy cannot emerge and endure. Of course truth is contested and never fully known or comprehended. It is the work of decades and centuries, and it involves both fact and judgement, reason and moral sentiments, ideas and the imagination. However, a sense of truth can develop over time, through the habitual formation of knowledge, the educative exercise of wise leadership, and the prudential adaptation in practice of previous example. A plural public debate requires a new internal ethos in order to promote the plural search for the common good while also protecting the institutions of democracy from the poisonous propaganda that corrodes liberty and free speech. Political debate has always been partisan and polarising, but much of it has taken place in the public realm and in plain sight. Now political argument is moving to the siloed space of social media with its online echo chambers that are largely impervious to scrutiny and accountability. The technology that ought to serve human needs and interests is being used to manipulate opinion and debase democracy.

If ethos is about quality and motivation, then one key task is to foster excellence and to nurture proper pride in a job well done. This lies deeper in human psychology than the mere pursuit of power, wealth or a shallow societal status. It is an inherently social motivation because it is linked to recognition by others for honourable performance of a mutually beneficial role. And here lies the core of a culture of genuine honour and nobility based on distinction – not inherited privilege or the power of an *arriviste* aristocracy denounced by Tocqueville. An alternative ethos would seek to instil the pursuit of self-worth as a pursuit of mutual recognition. In turn, this would encourage the search for truth and truthfulness in terms of facts and judgement, which also involves what the Canadian philosopher Charles Taylor calls 'social imaginary', defined as the 'ways people imagine their social existence, how they fit together with others, how things go on between them and their fellows, the expectations that are normally met, and the deeper normative notions and images that underline these expectations'.[29] Taylor's argument is that our lived experience has to conform considerably to the prevailing social imaginaries, otherwise democracy and the public realm will lack civic consent and popular participation. And when some of the informal norms of democracy – robust debate, viewing your opponent as a legitimate adversary rather than an enemy – are violated by elites in politics and the media, then the democratic process is not just fraying at the margins but faces an existential threat.

So, besides the economic break-up of monopoly power, what is needed is a renewed political architecture and social imaginary underpinned by a new ethos. Arguably there is a growing desire on the part of many people to combine cultural diversity with a stronger sense of common purpose and a shared sense of belonging. Where a minimum of rights and opportunities exist, one tends to start needing other markers of distinction, including forms of excellence and honourable action. And the more honour itself becomes a currency, the more both leaders and people will ally themselves through their choices to an honourable way of life. This can be achieved up to a point both through the internal ethos of politics and the media and through a new regulatory framework that demands a wider social purpose and civic responsibility. For example, persistent misinformation in the mainstream and the alternative media could lead to the loss of their legal licence, so that media organisations clamp down on wilful lying and deception. Where individuals or groups are explicitly targeted, the 'right to reply' should be extended in a spirit of free yet fair debate and robust argument.

The emphasis on ethos is closely connected with the idea of personal representation, which implies a strong fluidity between politics and civic education, since both are embedded in the interpersonal ties of society. Rather than imposing centralised control, a more 'personalised' government would grant under licence the performance of public functions to bodies of persons or to collective persons, which are corporations. Examples are universities and the BBC – despite growing managerialism and editorial bias. The universities' independence and yet public-spiritedness should today be renewed and upheld, and the BBC's role should be extended elsewhere via more regional and local outlets. Conversely, it is possible from this perspective to understand how 'self-appointed' educators and others are, nevertheless, carrying out 'political' functions to the benefit of the entire polity and even the state itself. But this does not imply that the state has no role. We need, rather, a new notion of the 'public' that slides between the purely private and the anonymous collectivity. It is here, at the centre of a programme for the renewal of democracy, that the idea of the strategic shaping of new institutions could stand – starting with a new royal college for journalists – but also a greater role for members in political parties, combined with limits on the power of groups to dominate the membership. The aim is at once to renew and democratise the role of 'the few', which means skilled elites at all levels of society that can uphold ethos and lead by example – a practice of virtue.

This can only come about alongside the strengthening of self-government for shared ends, as the following chapter will explore.

Virtue and greater self-organisation need first and foremost to become habitual through the growth of a new ethos internal to each institution. But, at the same time, they should at the limits of claimed infraction come within the purview of law and judicial debate. For example, the media regulator should have powers to hand out fines to those corporations such as Facebook and Google if they produce and distribute bogus stories in an attempt to attract attention and advertising but also to those click-hungry mainstream media outlets that persistently feature falsehoods by embedding on their websites links to lies. Printing insincere apologies on page 19 will not do. Beyond punishment, another mechanism to reduce demagogy is, as Matthew d'Ancona has suggested, to introduce a system of grading media sources 'according to their established credibility', with the worst offenders being flagged on a user's browser. Similar to Wikipedia, a combination of popular contribution and some level of quality control is necessary to ensure a better balance between free speech and a commitment to truth.

In conclusion: both politics and the media need a new ethos, but, while it can be encouraged at the political level through new incentives and rewards, in the end this change in ethos requires a cultural renewal. People cannot opt for what they have not been offered. The realism of renewal is that it must perforce begin among a minority, whose convictions can create the critical mass for majority consent if they begin to be successfully exemplified in practice – of which the outlawing of slavery and capital punishment in Europe are past examples. Just as success begets success, so too it is the case that good quality often prevails when it is actively promoted. For to do something right is also to do something well, which is how Aristotle defined the good that is internal to each human activity. To seek the good is to perform something in a manner that will achieve a greater end because virtues, such as courage and generosity, are mutually reinforcing and thereby able to endure over time. Truth inspires trust, and trust leads to further cooperation as high standards become the new norm. Of course lies and deception can corrode all this very quickly, but they also tend to inspire counter-movements. Faced with scandals such as the abuse of private data and election meddling, perhaps we are at the cusp of a backlash against social media manipulation. The renewal of democracy will have to involve political resolve and leadership to change the power nexus and promote a politics that is once more concerned with questions of substantive truth.

4

Anarchy – Atomisation and the Primacy of Association

1 The rise of post-democratic market-states

Liberal democracy replaces inherited status with natural equality before the law, which provides greater individual freedoms and rights, but the gains involved should not blind us to the losses linked to a progressive erosion of the social bonds and civic ties on which vibrant democratic systems depend for trust and cooperation. Democratic politics means greater equality of opportunity, but by the same token it is connected with societal fragmentation and, in recent years, levels of downward social mobility not seen since the 1920s. The promise of a democratic capitalism has given way to capitalist democracy, as I argued in chapter 2.

However, the key reason is not only the power of capitalism but also the tendency of liberal democracy to be atomistic, because liberalism's recognition of association and group identity is secondary to the recognition of individual rights that are ultimately upheld by the central state. As a result, the liberal priority of individual rights over group rights reinforces individualism by subordinating questions of mutual duties to the primacy of personal freedom as 'negative liberty' – i.e., the absence of constraints on free choice other than the law and private conscience. Responsibilities are seen as little more than a necessary consequence of rights – a small price we pay for our individual entitlements. Without a strong sense of obligation and shared social bonds, liberal democracy favours freedom over solidarity and individualism over reciprocity, which can be defined as the relationships of give and receive that underpin both interpersonal ties and the entire social fabric.

Furthermore, liberal democracy tends to oscillate between two poles of sovereign power: the sovereignty of the executive, with its oligarchic outlook, and the sovereignty of citizens as freely choosing individuals who are disembedded from ties of family, community and place and who entertain predominantly contractual connections with one another. What is lacking in liberal democracy is a positive, substantive conception of all the intermediary institutions, such as professional associations, trade unions, universities and free hospitals, that stand between these two poles – the mediating 'few' (elites at all levels) that bind together the sovereign 'one' (or ruler) with the sovereign 'many' (or people).[1]

The particular problem with contemporary democratic liberalism is that it undermines the autonomy of intermediary institutions in favour of oligarchic forces which threaten both the legitimacy of the 'one' and the sovereignty of the 'many'. Oligarchic power controls the executive branch of government while unleashing an ever greater anarchy of competing individuals in the marketplace, hollowing out the civic bonds that unite people as members of a shared polity.[2] There has been a marked decline in membership of civic associations and community-based institutions that help to constitute civic life.[3] Meanwhile the idea of being a citizen with obligations towards fellow citizens and the wider community is increasingly supplanted by notions of being a customer and client with demands vis-à-vis the state as a service provider. New forms of civic engagement have emerged, but the overall effect has been to weaken self-organisation and self-government as the institutions of state and market converge to dominate everyday existence.

This convergence of the central state with the global 'free market' has brought about the centralisation of power, the concentration of wealth and the commodification of social life that characterise contemporary liberal democracy. Over the past forty years or so, sovereign nation-states with liberal-democratic constitutions have morphed into globalised 'market-states' that exhibit illiberal and post-democratic tendencies.[4] After 1945, sovereign nation-states sought to embed the economy by providing public investment, universal welfare and full employment. By contrast, globalised market-states since the 1980s and 1990s have maximised client and consumer choice by opening up all levels of the economy to international finance, global free trade and mass immigration.

This shift in sovereignty from an international system of nation-states to a global order of market-states has coincided with a structural transformation of the world economy and global governance. There was a move away from the post-war Bretton Woods settlement of fixed exchange rates, regulated trade and capital controls towards the new emphasis on floating exchange rates, liberalised trade and ever higher capital mobility. In turn, this transformation further weakened the capacity of sovereign states to insulate their domestic democratic processes from international economic developments. In response, we have seen the rise of both the illiberal undemocratic liberalism of the ruling establishment and the anti-liberal direct democracy of political insurgents. What they share in common is a focus on globalisation and the nation-state, which ignores the central role of intermediary institutions in the realm of civil society.

There are three recent developments that highlight this omission. First of all, globalisation has simultaneously weakened national industries – as compared with transnational operations – and strengthened the role of international finance in distributing funds in search of maximal short-term returns. While it is true that multinational corporations and increasing global capital flows have undercut the power of sovereign states, it is also the case that government has often favoured this process by adopting policies of liberalisation, deregulation and privatisation. There have been important reasons for this in terms of the pursuit of economic prosperity. However, it suggests that states – especially large advanced economies such as the USA, the UK, the EU countries, Japan and certain emerging markets, including China and India – retain some considerable power and that there has been a certain convergence between 'big government' and 'big business'.

The historian Philip Bobbitt has described this convergence as the transition from the nation-state to the market-state.[5] The market-state is characterised by three paradoxes: (1) 'it will require more centralized authority for government, but all governments will be weaker'; (2) 'there will be more public participation in government, but it will count for less, and thus the role of the citizen *qua* citizen will greatly diminish and the role of citizen as spectator will increase'; and (3) 'the welfare state will have greatly retrenched, but infrastructure security, epidemiological surveillance, and environmental protection – all of which are matters of general welfare – will be promoted by the State as never before.' As Bobbitt concludes: 'These three paradoxes derive from the shift in the basis of legitimacy from that of the nation-state to that of the market-state.' Thus globalisation undermines both the social contract between citizens and their representatives and the underlying social imaginary (as discussed in chapter 3).

Second, economic liberalism has lifted millions out of poverty in emerging markets such as China or India and also provided new opportunities for many citizens in advanced economies. However, these same forces have left many traditional workers in the West jobless and worse off, both economically and in terms of self-esteem. From that perspective, the way liberal market forces based on freedom of choice, utility-maximisation and self-interest have been left to operate seems to have damaged the very fabric of society. As early as 1944, Karl Polanyi conceptualised the impact of economic liberalism in terms of the dual effect of first disembedding politics and the economy from society and then embedding social bonds in formal legal procedures and transactional ties.[6] There are counter-movements that seek to roll back the advance of market-state power. But, by the same token, capitalism functions within extra-capitalist spheres such as areas of social and cultural practice that remain external to an exclusively capitalist logic but sustain the operation of the market-state.[7]

Third, these extra-economic spheres include civil society organisations whose civic character is changed by their role in making capitalism more viable than would otherwise be the case. In consequence, many intermediary institutions of civil society have been progressively subsumed under the sovereign power of the central state, absorbed into the globalising tendency of the 'free market', or integrated into the system of global governance under the aegis of institutions such as the UN and its agencies – the World Bank, the IMF and the World Trade Organization – as well as supranational bodies such as the G7 or G20. Political power has tended to become more centralised and wealth more concentrated in many advanced economies. The ensuing lack of accountability, legitimacy and popular participation at the domestic level is part of the post-democratic tendency. Paradoxically, the dominant pillars of global governance have widened the gap between domestic democratic institutions and international economic decision-making, while at the same time reinforcing the dependence of everyday market economies upon transnational capital.

In this manner, market-states provide the conduit through which both political sovereignty and economic transactions are at the same time increasingly intertwined with one another and gradually uprooted from the social relations and civic bonds in which they are traditionally embedded along with the intermediary institutions of civil society. Of course there are a myriad of organisations that retain some degree of autonomy. But, as market-state power expands into new areas by an ever greater commodification of the natural world, education, the family and sex, civil society institutions are increasingly impotent. In everyday life people face greater economic interdependence but also greater social isolation than before. As the bonds of family, community, work, church and nation are eroding, the scale of loneliness and seclusion is growing.[8] We are connected with one another online, but often we lack real relationships in the places we inhabit. The social theorist Sherry Turkle has given this paradoxical phenomenon the apposite appellation 'alone together'.[9] With new levels of digital dependence and addictive attention-seeking, over-excitement and disenchantment cascade into each other. Instead of mutual recognition and flourishing anchored in notions of the common good, politics and social life become about power, wealth or social status reduced to individualised identity.

2 Liberal democracy's slide into atomism

Here one can go further than the notion of post-democratic market-states and make the point that contemporary liberalism, with its roots in classical liberalism, is irredeemably atomistic. It subordinates social ties to depersonalised values and abstract standards such as global economic exchange or top-down bureaucratic regulation. In this manner, liberal rule replaces the anthropological primacy of interpersonal trust and cooperation with the impersonal forces of individual right and formal contract that rest on the pessimistic ontology of the social contract tradition.[10] This applies not only to Thomas Hobbes's and John Locke's assumption of a violent 'state of nature' that requires the artificial order of state coercion and market competition. It also holds for Jean-Jacques Rousseau's idea of freely born individuals whose egoism (born out of comparison and rivalry with others) needs to be mediated by a social contract – enforced by national republics or a cosmopolitan federation of nation-states, as for Immanuel Kant.[11]

Either way, different social contract theorists share a gloomy outlook about the individual or the free association of people – or both at once. So if human beings (alone or in society) are selfish, greedy, distrustful of one another and prone to violence, then the impersonal institutions of state and market are best positioned to minimise conflict and maximise security, freedom and equality. The 'visible hand' of state coercion and the 'invisible hand' of market competition regulate human violence where the latter is seen as either naturally given or socially constructed, but either way as necessary and inevitable rather than as the outcome of historically contingent factors.[12]

Nor is this merely a theoretical point. The French Revolution illustrates the institution of this logic well. One of the first acts of the revolutionaries was to abolish all the intermediary institutions of civil society and re-create them under the absolute authority of the central state. The *Loi Le Chapelier* of 1791 banned the totality of guilds and fraternities (or *compagnonnage*) defended by figures such as Montesquieu. The law was followed by a decree on 18 August 1792 which dissolved all types of congregations, both of the clergy and of the laity – including universities, faculties and learned societies. Taken together, the law and the decree eliminated the right to strike and instituted enterprise as the most fundamental mode of association or corporation. That is why the revolutionaries did not put an end to the power of privilege, whether in the form of patronal clubs or monopolistic arrangements that were ultimately in league with the central state. From the outset, the bureaucratic statism of the French Revolution was complicit with the cartel capitalism that underpins *dirigisme* at home and mercantilist trade abroad. That is why Colbertism represents one of the numerous continuities between the *ancien régime* and the various models of republican France from the seventeenth century to the present day.[13]

These shifts in both ideas and institutions decisively shaped modern politics around the double sway over society of state and market. What emerges is the primacy of the political and the economic over the social. Government produces politically the commercial sphere of pure exchange and tries through the educative and other central institutional processes of 'civil society' – in a novel and specific sense – to create new citizens on the basis of inalienable, individual rights. The mark of modern, revolutionary citizens is to be negatively choosing, self-governing and disembedded from family, locality, tradition and artisanal formation – and so from civil society in an older, more generic sense.

If liberal democracies have experienced a growing centralisation of power and a concentration of wealth over the past forty years or so, then it has to do with the further expansion of both state and market power in hitherto autonomous, more mutually governed areas and the concomitant further retreat of intermediary institutions from their traditional involvement in economic, social, educational, cultural and charitable activities. Market monopolisation and market logic have ensured that the economy has become yet more dramatically disembedded from society in general. Meanwhile, the same process combined with government control has led to interpersonal relationships being subsumed yet further under either bureaucratic rule or commercial transactions – or indeed both at once.

Crucially, state and market have increasingly made this covert alliance explicit. The real political polarity now lies not between their respective degrees of influence but between their oligarchic collusion, on the one hand, and the realm of civil society, on the other. As already mentioned, this is an ambivalent term, but there is an older and more generic sense to indicate the 'complex space' of intermediate institutions that mediate between the individual, groups, the state and the market. Examples include self-governing hospitals, friendly societies, professional associations for manufacturing and trading, free universities, religious organisations, and multitudinous voluntary bodies organised round shared interests or charitable purpose, besides more informal social processes and groupings.

In this space, people can associate with one another – either as individuals or as members of groups and corporate bodies – in order to defend shared values and advance common interests. By contrast, the globalised market-state has subordinated the sanctity of labour, land and life to abstract values and standards, thereby reducing the dignity of the person to 'bare individuality' (Giorgio Agamben). Similarly, the shared quest for the common good has been discarded in favour of the private pursuit of either individual utility or subjective happiness such as short-term pleasure. Decades of liberalisation have provided greater opportunities for many and afforded some protection against the worst violations of the freedom of some by the freedom of others, especially given the growing disagreement about substantive notions of justice and the good life. However, economic liberalism has also undermined the civic and social bonds of association on which functioning markets and democratic debate depend. Cultural liberalism has underwritten the commodification of reality in terms of its commitment to liberation.

And, paradoxically, the two liberalisms have brought about a society that is not just more atomised but also more intertwined in the wrong way – too tied to the oligarchy of global finance and tech giants that dominate the everyday economy. The exponential growth in consumer and sexual freedom has become a kind of opiate that covertly reconciles people to the loss of civil liberties and self-determination at the workplace.

Perhaps even more paradoxical is the point that the supposed triumph of liberalism after 1945, and especially after 1989, is based on the liberal rejection of all utopian ideologies. However, this rejection ends in a utopian promotion of an anti-utopian project: the liberal order is now the only globally acceptable political, economic and moral order *precisely* because it purports to be the 'realm of lesser evil', as Jean-Claude Michéa has argued.[14] In reality, political liberalism has fixed the global ground rules for 'fair play' between independent human freedoms, while at the same time proscribing any substantive alternatives to those procedural rules and formalistic standards. In the name of neutrality that only liberal ground rules can secure, debates about the common good and the shared ends of human flourishing have been banished from the court of public political discussion.

This was first fully theorised by John Rawls and Ronald Dworkin, whose legalist philosophies posited that freedom can be codified into a fixed system of interlocking liberties that are no longer matters of political deliberation or cultural discussion but decisions for legislators and the judiciary.[15] This is the intellectual basis for a left-wing focus on individual human rights. Meanwhile the political right embraced the ideas of Friedrich von Hayek on protecting property and other private rights from democratic decision-making.[16] Either way, the left- and right-wing convergence around a rights-based liberalism enthroned the primacy of rights as entitlements over mutual obligation and thereby of the technocracy that enforces these individual claims over popular democracy.

Nearly two hundred years ago, Tocqueville warned about a lack of democratically self-governing association within liberal democracy:

> A government can no more be competent to keep alive and to renew the circulation of opinions and feelings among a great people than to manage all the speculations of productive industry. No sooner does a government attempt to go beyond its political sphere and enter upon this new track than it exercises, even unintentionally, an insupportable tyranny . . . . Governments therefore should not be the only active powers; associations ought, in democratic nations, to stand in lieu of those powerful private individuals whom the equality of conditions has swept away.[17]

111

3 The primacy of association

Political thinkers from Aristotle, via Edmund Burke and Alexis de Tocqueville, to Alasdair MacIntyre have argued that democracy needs to promote a balance of interests, so that it does not slide into either an unmediated anarchy of unfettered individualism or the coercive control of the people by an authoritarian oligarchy. Central to such a balance of interests are independent and democratically self-governing voluntary associations that can mediate between individuals and also counterbalance both state and market power. A civil society composed of strong intermediary institutions makes democracy less individualistic and anarchic and oriented more towards the common good – balancing individual fulfilment with mutual flourishing in ways that respect the equal dignity of all.

Civil society alone cannot resist the power of post-democratic market-states and the underlying atomistic liberalism. A transformation of the polity from anarchy to greater association requires a 'civil state' and a moral market that can democratise politics and the economy so that they will be embedded in the social relations of civil society institutions. Here it is instructive to build on the shared roots of Karl Polanyi's economic anthropology and Paul Hirst's idea of 'associative democracy',[18] which can be traced to nineteenth- and early twentieth-century critiques of liberalism and alternative theories of pluralism.[19] One key argument made by both Polanyi and Hirst is that the dominant forms of liberalism fuse individualism with collectivism in ways which weaken democratic self-government. Both *laissez-faire* capitalism and neo-liberal capitalism reduce not just goods and labour but also land and social relations to commodities that can be freely exchanged according to their monetary market value.

Bound up with this is the primacy of subjective, individual rights over mutual duties and reciprocal responsibilities within groups and associations. Since unbridled commercial exchange requires a force to eliminate resistance to it and compensate for any failures, liberal capitalism combines the 'free' market with the strong state. For example, statist welfare run centrally and based on uniform standards and targets is subservient to capitalism because it compensates for market failure but does not change the fundamental relation between capital owners and wage labourers.[20] As such, much of economic and political liberalism tends to combine market atomism with state corporatism.

The pluralist alternative to the liberal paradigm is to transform both capitalist markets and collectivist states in the direction of 'civil states' and moral markets that are embedded in the voluntary, democratically self-governing civic associations. Such associations cut across the false liberal divide between the purely private sector of utility-maximising profit and the exclusively public sector by cooperating with state authorities and market actors in the delivery of services such as health, education or welfare. As Paul Hirst puts it, this approach 'aims to strengthen government in and through civil society; thus civil society takes on many of the attributes of the public sphere.'[21] Political authority is more effective and democratic if it is decentralised in line with the principle of subsidiarity – devolving power to the most appropriate level that promotes democratic participation and protects the dignity of citizens.

By contrast with centralisation and exclusive central state power, pluralism shifts the emphasis to an association of anchor institutions that share power through cooperative links according to necessity and contingency – hospitals, universities, trade unions, employers' associations and local chambers of commerce. According to this model, the economy is run not according to the logic of 'free-market' competition or bureaucratic state planning but instead along more mutualist lines, where firms are governed jointly by investors, managers and workers and financial investment includes a social purpose.

Polanyi's prescient analysis of capitalism, with its tendency towards greed and commodification, is a key complement to Hirst's idea of associative democracy, which renews and extends older traditions of mutualism and the new liberalism of T. H. Green or L. T. Hobhouse, with its emphasis on personal flourishing nurtured by relationships of mutual help.[22] Taken together, these approaches can provide the intellectual foundations on which to democratise the market and mutualise the economy. Maurice Glasman puts this well:

> The paradoxical idea here is that the greater the diversity of democratic institutions that entangle capitalism in relationships based on knowledge and mutuality, the better the chances of releasing the energies of the workforce and generating growth. The more workers have power, the more efficient it is; the more that local communities engage in banking, the more sustainable the returns. This is about breaking the logic of short-term returns, which undermines long-term development. I think that associative democracy has therefore to be

complemented by a much more explicit notion of the possibilities and threats of capitalism, the logic of the market, and how to domesticate it.[23]

Faced with the ravages of oligarchical capitalism, democracy can be strengthened if it fully embraces the idea of subsidiarity. One way in which more citizens can have agency is through the relative self-government of regions and free, democratically self-governed associations. This should occur not just in their own interests but also in terms of what they can thereby contribute by example and influence to the political whole. What this might have to involve is some kind of constitutional convention with strong parliamentary and popular involvement tasked with setting out a complete rebalancing of power between capitals, on the one hand, and localities and regions, on the other.

Transforming a centralised, unitary state – such as Britain – into a federalised, plural polity would carry through the logic of devolution based on the principle of subsidiarity, which means locating powers at the level that is most appropriate for the dignity and flourishing of the person. This tends to be in lower tiers, such as regional or local government, neighbourhood councils and even the parish level, but it can of course require action at higher levels of supranational and global institutions for problems such as migration, cross-border crime, terrorism, environmental devastation and financial regulation. Thus devolution inwards, properly understood, also entails, as its logical inverse, extension outwards.

Conversely, if more liberal democracy has the effect of weakening civil society, then the real alternative is not just greater democratic representation but also stronger elements of participatory and associative democracy at lower levels, where citizens can take part in shaping decisions and even policy-making. There are two dimensions to this argument. In terms of principle, strengthening intermediary institutions means valuing each and every person, so that they can participate in free associations and economic vocation. By exercising influence through more participation at the workplace, intermediary institutions can bolster democracy in the economy. And, in terms of practice, a more associative form of democracy is able to achieve a greater balance of interests against the twin threats of oligarchy and anarchy. For example, a constitutionally guaranteed framework for cooperation between local business and local government can provide a more balanced economy based on vocational training provided by technical colleges, high entry qualifications for the labour market, regional banks, and an alliance of traditional craft skills with modern technology, as is the case in Germany and northern Italy, which are home to some of the most competitive companies. Such a model can help produce sustainable economic success as well as greater personal fulfilment.

4 Strengthening local self-government

Many people are not members of voluntary associations, and the role of intermediary institutions has declined, most clearly in the case of trade unions but also in other forms of self-organisation. Therefore the state at all levels has a key role in creating the space in which citizens can once more associate freely, whether through the law, through regulation or by establishing a new institutional balance. This could take the form of greater devolution of power to elected mayors combined with a new framework for economic governance involving employers' associations, trade unions and local government – including greater worker representation in the established service sectors, in the growing 'gig economy' and within companies. Many of the ideas in this section are aimed at centralised, unitary states such as the UK or Spain, but others apply more widely. Key to the success of stronger local government is a clear distribution of responsibility in relation to central government and accountability to citizens who want their elected representatives to do their jobs.

First of all, a renewal of greater local self-government has to involve elected mayors not just in cities and city-regions but also in towns and even villages, because meaningful local elections foster democratic debate and extend popular participation.[24] In France, for example, there are almost 37,000 mayors; irrespective of party affiliation, they are among the most respected politicians because their proximity to citizens tends to improve accountability and trust. Open primaries and a first-past-the-post voting system would open up competition beyond candidates of established political parties. Against the argument that people would ignore mayoral elections, one might mention in the British context the successful introduction of elected mayors in London and other cities with increasing levels of voter turnout.

A better alternative to unitary authorities (as in the UK), which are simple but remote from citizens, is to establish a bicameral model. This would be composed of a local assembly as the lower house that functions as 'democracy locational' and represents people as individual citizens. In addition, there would be a newly created upper house that functions as 'democracy vocational' and represents people according to their profession or trade. The natural institution for the upper house is the old guildhall, with its history of representing guilds and giving workers status and better conditions. A new, expanded and more democratic version would enable all the trades and professions to be represented – including those currently lacking representation, such as carers, cleaners, cooks, security guards and other service personnel. The two houses would jointly make decisions about local levels of taxation and spending – with the upper house scrutinising and amending proposed decisions and the lower house having primacy in case of disagreement.

Combining directly elected mayors with a bicameral local assembly would provide a better institutional platform on which to locate people- and place-based public-service provision – services that reflect local needs rather than a central 'one-size-fits-all' approach. Such a system would also enable a more effective integration of the competing and conflicting arms of central government that currently dictate to cities and determine the modalities of 'powerhouses' and mayoralties. Stronger, more devolved local government would also offer the opportunity of linking bottom-up, community-based solutions (care, welfare, training) to larger-scale models of delivery – for example, by bringing together voluntary associations and social enterprises under the guidance of the mayor, the assembly and local civil servants. In this manner, local government neither provides all public services itself nor outsources them all to the cheapest for-profit supplier but, instead, promotes more mutualist arrangements by connecting and coordinating different providers and stakeholders who associate more freely with one another.[25] Thus renewed associative democracy complements representative democracy in ways that contemporary liberalism does not offer.

There are concrete examples that combine universal entitlement with localised and personalised provision, including grassroots initiatives such as 'Southwark Circle' or 'Get Together' in London. Initiatives of this kind reject old schemes such as uniform state-administered benefits, expensive and privately run services, or purely voluntary 'befriending'. Instead of centrally determined target and standards, they propose models based on civic activity and community organising with the support of regional or municipal governments. Citizens join welfare schemes such as social care as active members who shape the service they become part of rather than being reduced to merely passive recipients of a monolithic, top-down model. Southwark Circle works on the principle that people's knowledge of their neighbourhood, community and locality is indispensable to the proper provision and delivery of welfare. Services are delivered involving civic participation, social enterprise (such as the company Participle) and the local council. In this way, intermediary models seek to blend individual and group agency with state action.

A more participatory politics, in which people have greater control over their lives through building democratic institutions that embed state and market power, could also involve empowering the lowest tiers, including the parish and neighbourhood councils – for example, in villages and towns that are too small to have a bicameral system. As Maurice Glasman has argued, 'The parish is an elemental aspect of our polity that has kept a hold on the popular imagination. More people describe the place they live in terms of the 1536 parish map than they do the administrative map of 2017. The parish, the county, the town and the city remain the fundamental units of attachment and affection.'[26] What is vital is to give the parish level some real powers, including housing and policing, and to associate the population to decision-making. Within a strong parish-based assembly, citizens and their representatives can build relationships of trust, cooperation and accountability, which can blend leadership with popular participation in new forms of direct democracy that do not involve referendums.

A core obstacle to greater popular participation is the sheer lack of time in an age of longer working hours, commuting and an increasing imbalance between job and family or friends. This echoes Oscar Wilde's quip that 'The trouble with socialism is that it takes too many evenings.' One answer might be a new statutory right for people to take time off work for civic participation, which would provide valuable experience while at the same time opening up some opportunities for work. Here it is also worth exploring ideas about a national civic service for the adult population, indigenous and immigrant – starting with the 18- to 25-year-olds, who could spend a year learning about the importance of civic ties and social obligation by doing important tasks – from caring, via community help, to canal clearing.[27] A range of tasks would improve mutual understanding about different struggles of everyday life – a better antidote to individualism and the atomisation of society than a universal basic income that induces people to sit back, relax and float off into the internet ether.

Besides the renewal of local self-government, centralised liberal democracies such as the UK, France or Spain also require greater regionalism if they are to become more democratic. This can include city-states or city-regions as well as an empowered regional governance system. Key to the success of renewed regional autonomy is to reconnect urban spaces to their rural surroundings wherever possible and thereby to break down the existing barriers and to rebalance the priorities away from urban and metropolitan towards suburban and rural areas. Regional representation requires not just proper constitutional recognition and political status. The crucial point is that regions, big or small, refract particular identities often with deep historical roots, for example counties in England. People do not feel any attachment to the North West, the North East or the South East, which were always artificial entities, but they have great affection for Yorkshire, Kent or Surrey.

Moreover, opposition to the creation of regional assemblies in England was the result of resistance to party-dominated processes more than a lack of belonging and identity. The trick is therefore to 'politicise' existing cultural attachments, and this could more easily emerge if regional assemblies became associated with local pride, increased economic development and popular involvement in shaping the civic character. A particular task is to find ways of linking villages and small towns to middle-sized towns that tend to form the chains of conurbations, especially in certain regions of Western countries such as the north of England. The wider point is that people's identity is plural and involves local, regional, national and often international layers.

To avoid augmenting existing inequalities between areas where wealthy people can devote time and resources to their local areas, the role of central government is vital in providing strategic investment and harnessing cooperation between estranged interests, especially capital and labour. The guiding principles for the relation between the state and local government are subsidiarity and solidarity – the most appropriate level for decision-making in accordance with the dignity of the person and a sense of reciprocal obligation between richer and poorer parts of a country (or an association of peoples and nations, such as the EU, Mercosur, the African Union or ASEAN). Instead of bureaucratic or managerial models such as the regulatory or entrepreneurial state, the alternative is a model whereby the different tiers of government replace the priority of process, procedure and policy with the primacy of people, place and politics. Institutions and relationships provide a more meaningful framework to search for shared interests than top-down decisions or loose networks.

5 Mixed constitution

More fundamentally, the problem with contemporary liberal democracy is the excess of liberalism and the deficit of democracy. By contrast, the ancient constitution, with its combination of liberty with equality, self-government with authority, and progress with tradition, provides a better framework for renewing the democratic promise. These paradoxical combinations

go back to the idea that a proper constitutional settlement is itself a fusion of the 'one', the 'few' and the
'many' – a mixed constitution wherein sovereignty is
shared between the ruler, who in some sense embodies
the unity of the political (the 'one'), groups and associations that represent different interests and participate
in the governance of the polity (the 'few'), and people
who give consent through electing their representatives
and holding them to account (the 'many'). An updated
form of the ancient 'mixed constitution' can prevent
democratic government from sliding either into the
debased popular will of illiberal popular democracies
or into the unaccountable power of the executive allied
to the interests of a few turned oligarchic in the case
of undemocratic establishment liberalism. Indeed, the
wisdom enshrined in the ancient constitution suggests
that no polity can avoid the interplay of decision by the
'one', advice by the 'few' and assent by the 'many'.
The liberal-democratic tyranny of voluntary servitude is
the oppressive collusion of the 'one' and the 'few' that
follows upon the specious claim to rule only in the name
of the 'many' in the sense of a majority without representing the wider public interest.

The idea of 'mixed constitution' involves a more
blended cooperation of powers at the centre rather
than an insistence on the strict separation of powers.
Paradoxically, a formal separation tends to fuse the
dominance of the executive with the power of a ruling
oligarchy (the 'few' turned corrupt) because it expands
the scope for lobbying and money in politics – as in
the USA but also more recently in France. By contrast,
a more 'mixed government' blends central with local
power, and this balancing provides a mutual check

without eventual usurpation by 'the one' or 'the few'. Central to this is the role of 'the few' – virtuous inspirers and leaders at all levels of society who are organised in the manifold intermediary institutions that compose civil society. Here it is important to stress that virtue is not at all the same as moralism, as if some people have a monopoly on moral righteousness and can simply tell everybody else how to behave. On the contrary, virtue is an anthropological reality because it is a habit or quality that enables human beings to pursue purpose. Virtue emerges from activities, each of which has its own finality – how to be a good parent, neighbour, worker or football player. To practise virtue is central to a person's individual fulfilment of their unique talents and vocation and also to mutual flourishing – the relationships that give people meaning.

The problem today is not 'elitism' in itself, as there are always elites vying for influence and hegemony. Rather, contemporary elites are not only corrupt (an inherent tendency even in different forms of representative government) but have also changed the system insofar as they lead by bad example – actively promoting greed and selfishness as if these were good or at least 'neutral' values. There is not even the pretence to be more virtuous and to be seen to be so. A system of mixed government rests on a constitution that tries to uphold a better balance of power and the formation of more virtuous elites at every level and in every field who operate not through manipulation but by educative guidance of persons and groups who are thereby encouraged to develop their own talents. There is a certain ambiguity, as virtue involves both the faithful transmission of received wisdom, knowledge and skill and the transgressive invention of new ideas. In this sense, an updated championing of virtue is itself an example of how the old is the new.

And one perennial problem is a lack of popular agency in an age when power and wealth have flown upwards. Therefore Britain and other Western countries require new constitutional settlements that recover the natural link of mixed government with modern traditions of sovereign pluralism and federalism. Whether at the level of over-centralised states such as the United Kingdom or Spain, or at the level of supranational groupings such as the European Union, what is needed is the equivalent of royal commissions or constitutional conventions with strong parliamentary and popular involvement tasked with setting out a complete rebalancing of power between capitals, on the one hand, and localities and regions, on the other. Transforming the centralised, unitary state into a federalised, plural polity would carry through the logic of devolution based on the principle of subsidiarity, which means locating powers at the level that is most appropriate for the dignity and flourishing of the person.

Reforming national and supranational institutions requires a much greater long-term international involvement on the part of traditionally reluctant countries, including the occasional isolationism of the USA and the UK, whose recent actions have failed to foster nation- and institution-building. Concretely, it involves not just strengthening local government and creating institutions that democratise both the local polity and the local economy (as sketched out in the previous section) but also building a stronger legislature that is necessary to hold the executive to account and to counterbalance a judiciary that has been emboldened by a new supranational class of judges and lawyers.

Crucially, parliament needs to be reformed along the following lines. First of all, to create constituencies that coincide with local identity as far as possible: these will be bigger than existing constituencies and, thereby, also contribute to the reduction of the size of lower houses of parliament. Second, to introduce some system of transferable votes that reflects the more complex preferences of voters (other than voting for a single candidate of a single party) and link this to multi-member constituencies (which existed in the past), such that citizens in the newly created larger constituencies can be represented by more than one member of parliament. Such a system would balance the need to maintain a connection between people and their representatives with the need to break the monopoly of the two big parties and open up politics to other candidates. Among other desirable reforms of parliament are (1) much more time to scrutinise government bills; (2) a new mechanism of reducing the sheer amount of legislation (e.g., for every new bill in one area, at least two or three existing ones should be scrapped or radically simplified); and (3) considerably higher salaries for MPs, to augment their prestige, but no expenses system, in order to avoid corruption.

In conclusion: the liberal primacy of the individual over groups has privileged a politics around individual rights and entitlements that does not have much to say about mutual duties or obligations. 'Rights without responsibilities' tend to reinforce individualism at the expense of solidarity. To make rights and entitlements a reality requires a central authority – the strong state – that can enforce them and act as the ultimate arbiter of rival claims. Taken together, individualism and collectivism undermine the autonomy of voluntary and democratically self-governed organisations that stand between individual citizens, on the one hand, and the institutions of the state and the market, on the other. In turn, this contributes to an atomisation of society and a weakening of civic bonds, which erodes trust, cooperation and a sense of shared identity. This is evinced by the decline of social capital and the collapse of community cohesion.

The alternative to post-democratic market-states is a civil state and a moral market based on a renewed civic covenant that blends political representation with greater civic participation. First of all, to pluralise the state involves not just decentralising political authority and central bureaucracy and devolving them to lower levels in accordance with the principle of subsidiarity. It also encompasses a much greater participation of groups and associations in the activities of the public sector. For example, associations could provide a wide range of public services by forming cooperatives and mutuals that use state funding to deliver education, health care or welfare. By contrast with free-market managerialism or bureaucratic statism, such associations would focus on members – 'owners' (e.g., regional or local government), workers and users.

Moreover, the pluralisation of the state extends to national industries or publicly controlled utilities by establishing public-interest and community-interest companies. Like cooperatives or employee-owned businesses, such companies operate on the basis of mutualist principles that involve in their governance owners, workers and users. Public- or community-interest companies pursue not just private profit but also social ends by reinvesting their profits in the business and in the community instead of simply enriching the top management or institutional shareholders. Here, as elsewhere, the building of political and economic associations is an alternative to both liberal anarchy and market oligarchy.

A genuine alternative to liberal democracy also requires a mixed constitution, which is based on the enduring principles of freedom under the law and public cooperation as part of a constitutional covenant between the generations. Such a framework continues to offer resources to build a polity that pluralises politics and embeds both state and market into an extended public realm, a renewed civic covenant that views people not as contracting individuals but as members of a community of destiny – from the locality to the nation and beyond – in a double rejection of nationalism and atavistic ethno-centrism as well as of the suppression of regional identities and local self-government. By contrast with the liberal-democratic market-state, ancient mixed government sees society as primary and seeks to strengthen voluntary associations that can embed the institutions of state and market. The overarching aim is to pluralise the state and mutualise the market and embed them into the associative ties of civil society. Such a conception of democracy respects our nature as social, political beings who pursue mutual recognition and association around shared ends, which makes us more fully human.

5

Tyranny – Voluntary Servitude and Humanism

1 *Liberal democracy's slide into the tyranny of 'voluntary servitude'*

The primacy of the state and the market over human association can lead to a democratic system that instils a sense of voluntary servitude – a form of subtle manipulation by ostensible consent whereby people subject themselves freely to the power of the ruling oligarchy. The institutions of the central administrative state and global 'free market' regulate the 'naturally given' (but in reality merely assumed) anarchy, which is exacerbated by the lack of associative ties that leave citizens atomised. Tocqueville anticipated how liberal democracies based on mass opinion and self-interested representatives lack education in virtue and bonds of association, which engenders a novel form of tyranny that is neither ancient despotism nor modern dictatorship but, rather, a kind of subtle servitude based on tutelary power that bends our will.

Today liberal democracy is once more descending

into this tyranny of voluntary servitude as a result of liberalism's 'end of history' hubris and utopian outlook. The metaphysics of progress refracts into an embrace of historicism and a blind belief in historical laws, exemplified by the liberal Whig conception of history as evolving towards individual emancipation and social progress based on the expansion of capitalism. In consequence, all political and social institutions have to conform to capitalism's commodifying logic, which requires social engineering and the opening up of the family, communities, professional associations, the civil service, diplomacy and government to the joint forces of the unfettered market and the administrative state. Both politics and society are now subject to a process of abstraction from rootedness in place, tradition and nature that replaces the ancient idea of the 'self-government of the people', not simply with the communist 'administration of things' but with the hyper-liberal notion of 'governance by number'[1] – a managerial revolution based on technology that lays the foundation for a new anti-humanism.[2]

I will return to the anti-humanist thinking in today's liberal democracies in this chapter. For now, Tocqueville's warning about a slide into voluntary servitude applies to the promotion by contemporary liberalism of free choice, which progressively narrows the remit of what is permissible as the expansion of individual freedoms leads to ever more draconian limitations on collective agency – from the workplace, via the community, to the country. The liberalism of personal rights that trump mutual obligations has morphed into an all-consuming ideology. Behind a façade of equality, diversity and inclusiveness, it enforces uniformity, sameness and the exclusion of critics who are dismissed as reactionary – for example feminists questioning transgender ideas. In liberal democracies, it seems that everything can be debated publicly, including the private sphere, except the dangers of liberalism – hence the liberal attacks on free inquiry and free speech in the name of 'tolerance'.

Nowhere is this more clearly visible than in the liberal belief that the world cannot be accepted as it is and that the old must be replaced with the new. The roots of this creed go back to the origins of the modern era, with its rejection of the past and obsession with the future. From Machiavelli, via Descartes and Hobbes, to Bacon, the makers of modernity viewed the supposedly Dark Ages with a mixture of contempt and condescension.[3] They sought to inaugurate a new age in which man as the measure of all things and the highest rational animal would be master over nature. Human self-assertion went hand in hand with the subordination of mutual obligations to subjective entitlements, individual independence and national sovereignty. There is much gain involved but also the loss of tradition, belonging and common purpose. At the hands of liberalism, freedom becomes debased and descends into the vacuity of modernisation and the delusion that 'things can only get better'. The liberation from old bonds makes us richer but more divided, freer but lonelier. Paradoxically, the reverse face of 'negative freedom' is self-censorship and compliance with the liberal-democratic consensus underwritten by capitalism, statism and globalisation.

Moreover, 'negative freedom' makes us defenceless and malleable just because it rules out from the court of public discussion any discussion about shared ends around which we can associate. On the contrary, contemporary liberalism intensifies earlier strands going back to Hobbes, Locke, Kant and Rousseau about the replacement of the good with rights and the social contract and the argument that, in a context of value pluralism (Isaiah Berlin), we can only 'agree to disagree' and settle for Kantian ground rules of fairness (John Rawls) or discursive reason (Jürgen Habermas). Either way, procedure replaces purpose. This conception rests on the belief in originally 'self-possessed' individuals who are mutually contracting to ward off the threat of the other and thereby to conserve by artificial means their supposedly natural self-possession. In this sense, the liberalism underpinning liberal democracy remakes humankind in its own totalising image – a self-fulfilling prophecy foretold in *1984* and *Brave New World*. Eric Voegelin showed more than half a century ago that any political philosophy which seeks to replace lived reality with its own utopian imaginary is bound to descend into totalitarianism – whether the despotism of dictatorship or more subtle forms of tyranny.[4] Either way, representative democracy is being hollowed out.

Contemporary liberalism exacerbates the inherent tension between freedom and equality that characterises the very idea of democracy, as Raymond Aron – drawing on Tocqueville – reminds us.[5] Individual liberty and the equal status of all before the law are rival principles, and democratic politics involves a continual judgement about how to balance both and also blend them with the principle of fraternity. In the words of Danny Kruger, 'Fraternity is the sphere of belonging, of membership, the sphere of identity and particularity. It concerns neighbourhood, voluntary association, faith, and all the other elements of identity that relate us to some and distinguish us from others.'[6] Much of liberal thinking since the 1960s has shifted the balance in favour of an egalitarian politics that replaces the economic with the cultural redistribution of power within old elites and new classes rather than between social groups. Equality becomes debased and means little more than sameness – conformity with supposedly universal but in reality narrowly liberal values. Notions of diversity or inclusiveness are tools of intolerance that undermine free speech and rule out non-liberal values such as fraternity and reciprocity from the public political debate.

Both egalitarianism and oligarchic rule undermine the democratic representation of different interests within the framework of a parliamentary contest. Once more the root of this is the oppression that is involved in liberalism's focus on negative freedom to the exclusion of positive liberty. In the words of Aron,

> But if one retains only one criterion, that is one exclusive definition of freedom, one will arrive either at the paradox of an oppression that is recognised as legitimate in the name of the democratic process or at the paradox of a liberation that is decreed oppression because one refuses to compare the freedoms that some lose with those that others gain.[7]

The imbalance in favour of individual freedom to the detriment of a genuinely equal status of all suggests that liberal democracy is not so much periodically in crisis as permanently caught in an irreconcilable tension. This tension is not just between liberty and equality but also between rival conceptions of these two founding principles. Liberty oscillates between the positive freedom of self-government and the negative freedom of democratic

133

liberation that ends in a tyranny of voluntary servitude. Meanwhile, equality oscillates between equality before the law and the egalitarian debasement that ends in an oligarchy of power, wealth and social status, as Tocqueville first diagnosed. Liberal democracy's slide into 'democratic despotism' is therefore neither an accident nor a fatalism but an evolution that is inscribed into the very logic of democratic rule – an inversion of democracy that preserves an illusion of freedom and equality. Therefore the struggle is not so much for democracy against dictatorship as for a democracy that upholds the balance between a rich conception of freedom and equality against a democracy that debases them and thereby descends into oligarchic tyranny.

At the heart of this struggle is the question of the purpose of democratic rule – the distribution of power among individuals and groups with different yet also overlapping interests as well as the association around shared ends, such as the good life. Liberal democracy combines procedural ground rules with an appeal to abstract ideals such as emancipation or social justice. Both ground rules and abstract ideals ring hollow because they often overlook the relationships with family, friends, colleagues or fellow citizens, which provide substance to otherwise vacuous values. Liberalism's tendency towards economic oligarchy and social egalitarianism undermines a proper balance between personal freedom in the sense of the free pursuit of substantive purposes and social stability in the sense of cohesion among the members of a shared polity.

Human flourishing and joint well-being depend less on state regulations and economic contract than they do on mutual duties, about which contemporary liberalism has little to say. The same goes for moral and social virtues – courage, generosity, gratitude, loyalty, fraternity – that nurture the way we live in society. The liberal thinking that dominates representative democracy narrowly defines human beings in terms of their own self-ownership and their ability to contract with each other. Such a conception brackets out of the equation a genuine contest for the meaning of politics: what makes us social, political beings and, by extension, what makes us human?

2 The rise of transhumanism

The question of our humanity is once more coming to the fore of contemporary politics. The political insurgency that is sweeping through Western liberal democracies is often described as a form of anti-establishment populism that enlists support from those 'left behind' by globalisation. Other than that, the far left around Jeremy Corbyn, Syriza and Podemos and the alt-right around Donald Trump and kindred leaders seem to have little in common with each other. But this ignores the shared philosophy that underpins the resurgent extremes – a curious mix of libertarian tech utopianism and authoritarian statism that not only seeks hegemony but also wants to redefine human nature.

The surrender of humanism is at the heart of a new politics around which the hard left and the radical right converge – a politics that gives up on work, place and institutions in favour of leisure, cyberspace and networks. Instead of human labour and creativity, technological innovation and algorithms will govern the economy, while a transnational 'multitude' will replace both the working class and sovereign nation-states.[8] Citizenship and democratic resistance against state-backed capitalism will give way to the new leisure class of passive consumers living off a universal basic income (see chapter 2). On all this right libertarians in Silicon Valley and the European hard left agree. Their shared utopianism claims to invent the future, but it returns politics to anti-humanist traditions.

Today's tech utopians view technology not simply as an engine of economic growth or social advancement. Rather, technological innovation offers the opportunity of 'human enhancement', which aims to upgrade physical and mental performance, eliminate the process of ageing and even overcome mortality. This utopia threatens to abolish the humanist commitment to the equal value and dignity of all human beings whatever their physical attributes or intelligence. Genetic manipulation, the fusion of humans with machines, and artificial intelligence raise the prospect of different categories of human beings and the emergence of a post-human species. All this is reminiscent of the eugenics movement pioneered by Francis Galton, a cousin of Charles Darwin's who, upon reading *On the Origin of Species*, asked: 'Could not the race of men be similarly improved? Could not the undesirables be got rid of and the desirables multiplied?' Then, as now, the desire to transcend our human condition of being vulnerable and mortal is driven by a blind belief in the categorical goodness of science and progress. The utopian claim is that scientific advancement is always good and that it will accelerate social and ethical progress.[9]

But, just as history is contingent and discontinuous, so too is progress conditional and reversible. What is gained can be lost. Advancement involves both development and decline. Technological innovation is profoundly ambivalent, as it has empowered individuals and improved their lot but has also been an instrument of domination and undone advances in civilisation. The whole idea of linear, boundless progress is an Enlightenment myth grounded in the fiction that only a society governed by modern science could defend humankind against the enemies of reason. Yet this fiction rests not on science and rationality but on fanatical scientism and a Jacobin-style revolutionary politics to transform what it means to be human. From Robespierre via the eugenics movement to Stalin, the Nazis and Mao, history since the onset of modernity refutes the claim that the Enlightenment ideal of progress has produced all the advances of the modern era and none of its barbarism.[10]

Contemporary politics risks returning to this anti-humanist position in a new guise. The hard left and the radical right are embracing technological determinism to promote a new anti-humanist utopia that rests on the same logic of rejecting natural law, fetishising transgression and embracing the nihilism of 'dark enlightenment' disguised as a liberating tech utopia.[11] In this they are amplifying certain strands of liberalism (as I will show below). Rejecting the liberal model of capitalist globalisation, the resurgent extremes seek to institute an alternative modernity that is anti-liberal and simultaneously an intensification of certain liberal ideas: the cult of the individual, an invocation of the 'will of the people', the unmediated power of technology, and a vision of the universe in which nature and humanity will be governed by a new Promethean spirit.[12] Prometheanism combines a naturalist philosophy in which reality has no purpose with a materialist politics driven by economic-technological forces – a belief it shares with the accelerationist Marxism of the hard left.

Just like Prometheus' theft of fire sought to subvert the power of the gods in an attempt to raise up humans from their supposed humiliation, so too the new Prometheanism attempts to remake humanity through the unmediated power of technology. The convergence of nanotech, biotech, infotech and cognitive science serves to create a 'plane of closed immanence' that transcends our human condition in the direction of a new 'singularity', which is grounded in a flat ontology of equivalence between all subjects that make up the 'multitude' (Michael Hardt and Antonio Negri). The aim is to liberate the individual and the masses not simply from the trap of contemporary capitalism but, above all, from any limits of nature or history.

Both the natural order and inherited traditions are seen as arbitrary, irrational boundaries on our free mind, which artificially creates reality from nothing. In this manner, technologically enhanced humanity replaces the Creator God or some notion of divine transcendence as the source of being. Instead of coming into existence *ex nihilo*, humans are now revealed to have a 'will to nothingness', which paradoxically is the ultimate ground of everything – all techno-scientific possibilities. The nihilist core of Promethean thinking reduces the realm of immanence to the unmediated power of the individual that seeks nothing other than self-aggrandisement and the affirmation of pure will without any mediated relationship to others or to nature. Transhumanism is a nihilism. In the words of Ray Brassier, 'existence is worthless ... and nihilism is ... the unavoidable corollary of the realist conviction that there is a mind-independent reality which ... is indifferent to our existence and oblivious to the "values" and "meanings" which we would drape over it in order to make it more hospitable.'[13]

The Promethean spirit promises to release us from our affections and attachments to relationships and institutions that make us more fully human as social, political beings. That is what Brassier means by 'nihil unbound'. Such a release is not the same as liberation from oppression and exploitation combined with a promotion of human self-government, which were historic concerns of left and right. Rather, Brassier and his fellow accelerationists have in mind what they call in their manifesto 'a Promethean politics of maximal mastery over society' (§21). Here libertarian freedom meets totalitarian control, which fuses 'the command of The Plan' with 'the improvised order of The Network' (§14). This means not resisting or transforming capitalism but instead realising the capitalist utopia of infinite possibility based on an ontology of immanence: 'expansion beyond the limitations of the earth and our immediate bodily forms' (§22) '... towards the universal possibilities of the Outside' (§24). Only accelerationism, so the argument goes, can fulfil the promise of the Enlightenment to 'shift beyond the world of minimal technical upgrades towards all encompassing change' (§22),[14] because humanity and the universe are by nature deficient and require technological completion. The individual, released from all constraints, can be whatever he or she wants.

3 Identity politics and the resurgence of anti-humanism

If these ideas have political purchase, it is because contemporary politics is obsessed with individualised identity, as I argued in chapter 3. Identity politics takes the Enlightenment principles of individual will and 'man as the measure of all things' to the next level. The historical concern of politics with nurturing citizenship and forming character was lost through a slide into moralism and an obsession with the idea of an 'unencumbered self', which is at once more dependent on others yet more atomised – freer but lonelier (as discussed in chapter 4). Real relationships in the place people inhabit are increasingly replaced by virtual connections online. It is not just addiction to the web and the sheer time we spend in cyberspace rather than the real world.

The even more worrying trend is the demand for robot companions that are seen as more desirable than fellow human beings. We embrace robots as teachers, carers and even lovers just as we keep humans at a distance.[15] Relationships with embodied beings are mediated by machines, which allow us to escape any unwanted human contact with a simple click – divert calls, block messages and 'unfriend' people on social media. Fear of reality unmediated by technology goes hand in hand with an elite-promoted preference for simulations of life over life itself. As interaction with machines becomes a substitute for relationships with flesh-and-blood people, we put our faith in technology as a panacea for human frailty when acceptance of frailty is what makes us more truly human.

Today the humanist basis of politics and culture is once again under threat. Both the radical right and the hard left fuse technological determinism with their brands of identity politics that speak competing anti-humanist languages. On the left, we are seeing a celebration of the further blurring of the boundaries between genders, between childhood and youth, between casual and committed, and between human, animal and machine. All these blurrings will increase human unhappiness by eroding the relationships of affection and attachment on which we all rely in our everyday life. Casual jobs and casual sex are celebrated as virtuous examples of individual self-expression, whereas stable, meaningful work and enduring faithful love are portrayed as an outmoded repression of our negative freedom. The casualisation of life is both a source and a reflection of atomisation and narcissism.[16]

In response, in contemporary liberal democracy the double hydra of state and market will assume ever greater control over processes of human reproduction, economic production, leisure, education and culture. The purpose of knowledge is now to accelerate the process of automation in the direction of liberty, comfort and happiness for the global multitude – not just the few. These ideas shape far-left projects such as 'fully automated luxury communism'.[17] Party and parliamentary democracy are replaced by what Jon Cruddas has called 'cyborg socialism' – a fusion of utopianism with hyper-liberal cosmopolitan identity and transhumanism.[18]

On the right, we are witnessing an injection of 'alt-right' themes into the mainstream, of which Trumpism is the prime example. There is a return of 'race' as a supposedly objective category, with an accompanying legitimation of racial stereotyping and racial preference. Donald Trump may have disavowed people such as Richard Spencer who call for ethnic cleansing in order to protect what he describes as the 'dispossessed white race'. But Trump's defence of far-right counter-protesters against the removal of Confederate statues in Virginia and his endorsement of the racist Alabama senate candidate Roy Moore suggests a deeper sympathy for alt-right ideas.[19] The Trump administration's (now abandoned) policy of separating children from parents who are caught crossing the US border without a permit in the name of its 'zero tolerance' approach to illegal immigration shows just how brazen the attacks on the family are. Trump's attempt at state capture to smash the establishment has strengthened the 'big government' that it promised to abolish. His ideology is anti-conservative because he is entrenching the power of corporate money in politics and consolidating the oligarchic hold over democracy.

The far left and the radical right fundamentally disagree on immigration, multiculturalism and taxation, but they nevertheless converge around an anti-humanist agenda of libertarian release and authoritarian tyranny. Libertarian capitalists rail against the regulatory powers of central government even as they subject their workers to ever harsher production targets and invasive performance measures and lobby legislators in order to weaken organised labour further. The revolutionary left wants to replace the working class with machines and labour with leisure financed by taxing the tech giants. In each case, big government and big business collude at the expense of parliamentary democracy, worker self-organisation and local self-government, which in theory, and often in practice, have shown greater regard for the dignity of the person.

Even the more mainstream left has embraced the idea of acceleration as the latest mode of social engineering. 'Move fast and break things', as Mark Zuckerberg, the founder of Facebook, seems fond of saying.[20] The monopoly power of the tech giants not only eliminates market competition but also undermines democratic debate by controlling access to knowledge. Silicon Valley and big finance on Wall Street form an oligarchy that combines disruption with dispossession. Connecting the libertarian left with the libertarian right is an unabashed social Darwinism that privileges individual will and the power of the strong. The real 'left behind' are those who value being human more than being economically useful or technologically malleable. By contrast, contemporary social Darwinists reject any notion of a balance in nature and society in favour of control by a techno-oligarchic vanguard. In their shared worldview, the impersonal forces of technology will dominate our everyday existence and redefine what it means to be human. The humanism around which Western civilisation and liberal democracy were built is being replaced by a transhuman dystopia.

But anti-humanism is not confined to the political extremes. Based on a similar Promethean spirit, liberals have passed laws permitting euthanasia and sex changes for minors without parental agreement – as in Belgium, the Netherlands and Norway. To allow people to die as they wish or to change their gender is to subordinate the intrinsic value of human life to freedom of choice and the pursuit of individual happiness,[21] itself reduced in utilitarian fashion to the maximisation of pleasure and the avoidance of pain – not a richer sense of happiness that combines personal fulfilment with mutual flourishing. Since we are born into specific bodies and cultures at particular moments in time, the notion that our whole life is or should be purely a function of our own volition is misguided. To make it a matter of choice is to encourage the wider liberal and capitalist illusion that the human subject is an empty will, detached from her body of which she is the mere proprietor. There are very few people who feel neither male nor female, and while their difference should be recognised, exceptions tend to prove the rule that gender occurs exhaustively as male or female. Furthermore, to acknowledge historical and natural limits on our bodies includes the acknowledgement that life involves dying and some measure of suffering, however difficult it is to accept this for our loved ones or ourselves. What makes us human and happy is now understood once again in utilitarian terms as maximising pleasure and avoiding pain, and liberals who claim we have a right to happiness abhor the thought of human frailty because it gets in the way of feeling good about yourself.

The liberal conception of happiness also violates a universal ethical principle that has governed most cultures and societies in history – nature and human life have almost always been recognised as having a sacred dimension beyond the power of human volition. No person enjoys full sovereign jurisdiction over his possession of life and his body. The dominant strands of liberalism redefine life as something that belongs to individuals as their own property, echoing Locke's anthropology of humankind as self-proprietary.[22] But even self-ownership requires protection by the state, and therefore liberalism effectively grants government power over life itself. That is why many liberals have not hesitated to liberalise euthanasia, which hands over life to the individual, who is uprooted from relationships and self-governing institutions and who is ultimately dominated by state and market forces. Life for liberals is a commodity that can be traded or dispensed with without regard to its intrinsic worth. A liberal democracy that rests merely on procedural ground rules and the supreme value of negative freedom is unable to resist this commodification.

If life has no intrinsic worth, then we would have to conclude that we really are isolated individuals, disembedded from interpersonal relationships with other embodied beings and reducible to biological-chemical processes. To adopt this naturalist perspective is to abandon the entire basis of Western humanism and to replace the idea of dignity with private liberty or comfort, which are now the only constraints on individual choice as they stop people from harming others but not from engaging in self-harm. Paradoxically, contemporary liberalism promises release from any constraint not chosen by consenting individuals who have no obligation to anyone. At the same time, people are increasingly subordinate to an overweening state and the unfettered free market.[23] Liberal man is the freest man ever to have lived and at the same time the most domesticated (Pierre Manent). Here one can go further than Manent to suggest that domestication is a denial of our animal nature and our condition as *homo faber* – the ambiguity between conservation and creativity. The human longing and yearning for meaning makes us spiritual beings in ways that the materialist thinking of liberalism cannot recognise. Liberal man is materially the richest and at the same time spiritually the most dispossessed.

Libertarians and liberals converge around the notion of liberty as free choice and the pursuit of individual happiness. This is understood as including the right to terminate the lives of the elderly or the suffering. What is legitimated here is not a genuinely desirable democratic right but instead the will to power of some over others and essentially the strong over the weak. If the unique value of each human person is not upheld, then nothing prevents ending the lives of children and adults deemed to be too ill or too frail. This is an updated version of social Darwinism under the guise of liberal choice. Ironically, the science-based 'enlightened' liberalism ends up on the same side as the Nietzschean will-to-power that liberals such as Steven Pinker in his book *Enlightenment Now* associate with all the evils of modernity.

We are already at the point where the humanist foundations of equality and dignity are under attack from an unholy alliance of elites and insurgents. Both libertarian and liberal thinking point towards a new form of biological totalitarianism based on a refusal of all value except the will of the strong individual. Frailty is now considered a threat to the human race in a way that exceeds Nietzsche's critique of Christianity as a philosophy of weakness and transvaluation. The tyrannical demon of liberal democracy takes the form of neo-utilitarian calls to strip human life of its sanctity by extending euthanasia to 'severely and irreparably retarded infants' and those forms of human and non-human life whose medical condition causes 'suffering to all concerned and benefits nobody'.[24] Belgian legislation to make assisted suicide available to minors, even against the express wishes of the parents, is but the latest example of new nihilist norms.

Neither the liberal centre nor the resurgent extremes have learned the lessons of Aldous Huxley's warnings about totalitarian temptations in *Brave New World*. A control over reproduction is now more easily attained through self-release and promiscuity than self-discipline and fidelity. This allows the state to deal with the individual directly rather than through the mediation of couples and families, which can offer more resistance to central intervention. Much of liberal feminism and minority rights activism too readily colludes with this underlying reality. These movements also embrace the commodification of human reproduction, which becomes a matter of contractual exchange – as with surrogacy.[25] Precisely because such matters raise complex ethical questions, economic-social liberalism, with its cult of pure individual rights or a covert denial of human dignity, is insufficient. Moreover, it is too rarely noticed that sexual permissiveness has today, as Huxley already noted in his dystopian novel, become a kind of opiate that covertly reconciles people to the loss of other freedoms – at the workplace, in the locality and beyond.

This is neither to overlook real social progress nor to forget that all remaining discrimination is a denial of human equality on which humanism depends. At the same time, greater personal autonomy coincides with a growing sense of people's powerlessness. Liberalism and libertarianism have liberated us from bonds of family, community and nation, but the impersonal mechanisms of state and market that have replaced those interpersonal ties leave most of us at once freer yet lacking in agency. The vision of humanity shared by liberals and libertarians offers freedom of choice yet subordinates people to forces that cannot be governed democratically and that disregard dignity and human flourishing. These are themes that appeal not only to religious people but also to all those who are spiritually sensitive and worry about rampant individualism and materialism. Yet behind the isolated individual always stands the state. It can either give in to totalitarian temptations or, on the contrary, uphold principles that grant human existence a unique status. It can either promote death or choose life. The defence of humanism is the new pivot in politics, and democracy can go either way. If politics chooses life, it will more likely have the cultural strength to confront democracy's demons.

Conclusion – Renewing the Democratic Promise

In 1997 the American commentator Fareed Zakaria wrote an influential essay in *Foreign Affairs* on illiberal democracy in which he argued that 'the two strands of liberal democracy are coming apart . . .. Democracy is flourishing . . . liberalism is not.'[1] While this evolution might have applied to some of the former transition countries, the more significant development has been just the opposite – the rise of hyper-liberalism and the erosion of democracy. This excess of liberalism and the deficit of democracy lead to a lack of legitimacy as growing economic and cultural insecurity, combined with social fragmentation, undermines the social contract that is the bedrock of liberal democratic government. In the final instance, liberal democracy is caught in a tension between the positive freedom of popular self-government and the negative freedom of ever greater individual choice and between an equal status of all before the law and the reduction of equality to sameness. Liberal democratic models are self-eroding as they conjure up the demons of oligarchy, demagogy, anarchy and tyranny.

Conclusion

Across the West and beyond, countries have witnessed the rise of undemocratic illiberal liberalism and an anti-liberal insurgency that are but two sides of the same coin. Both are mutually reinforcing and define their legitimacy in opposition to each other: elite technocrats claim to guard against anti-elite insurgents who seek to overthrow the establishment that is seen as corrupt and out of touch. But in reality both involve oligarchic power and deploy a mix of authoritarianism with populist demagogy. They invoke the primacy of the will over any other principle – whether the primacy of individual volition or the 'will of the people'. Liberalism and populism also concentrate power and wealth in old elites and new classes turned corruptly oligarchic. They undermine parliamentary democracy and are silent about what people share as citizens or what binds them together as members of national and cultural communities. Both polarise politics and further divide society just when democracy requires a transcendent conversation about how in a context of plural values we can forge a common life.

This will require far more than either restating liberal democracy's founding values of liberty and equality or delivering on the promise of prosperity and peace. Rather, democracy requires a renewed civic covenant – what Edmund Burke called 'partnership . . . not only between those who are living, but between those who are living, those who are dead, and those who are to be born.'[2] This emphasis on covenantal ties among generations can help us address the growing economic injustice between young and old today. Society is not a contract of individuals but a partnership between the generations that balances individual rights with mutual obligations and contributions with rewards. But today we have a culture of entitlement that does just the opposite. Workers who have contributed for a lifetime receive 'nothing for something' – the same meagre unemployment benefits as the young or migrants who get 'something for nothing'. Justice without compassion is empty, just as compassion without justice is blind. The path towards greater economic justice involves a renewed balance of interests among the generations and the building of a common good between estranged parts of the body politic.

Covenants endow social relations with meaning that is missing from Hobbes's and Locke's idea of social contract underpinning liberal democracy because it ignores our social nature. Human beings are not atomised agents maximising their utility. Nor are they anonymous carriers of historical laws. We are born into social relations, 'the little platoon we belong to in society' (Burke), and these are the first object of our affections. We learn to love and care for family, neighbours, friends, colleagues and fellow citizens. Far from being confined to the in-group, this love creates a sense of attachment and belonging that extends to strangers – 'the strangers in our midst' who become part of our communities.[3]

Liberal elites and anti-liberal insurgents have little to say about our social nature. We are embodied beings who are embedded in relationships and institutions. They command affection and forge attachment as they are rooted in people's identity and interests. These 'public affections', as Burke called them, are indispensable to the good functioning of the rule of law. They build trust and cooperation on which a prosperous market economy and a vibrant democracy depend. An appeal to love and affection reflects the primacy of relationships over impersonal mechanisms. The practice of lived fraternity can shape a politics of affection and attachment to people, place and purpose. This primacy of real relationships extends from the domestic arena to international relations. The strongest partnerships forged between nations come not through treaties or trade but through cultural association, and democracy within and between nations cannot survive and flourish without it.

We live in troubled times. A sense of anger and abandonment is spreading as people feel humiliated, unable to live the lives they hope for and powerless to shape the forces that dominate them and those they care about most. Politics is about nurturing a sense of fraternity – lived solidarity that can mediate between liberty and equality and direct collective action towards a plural search for the common good. A middle path of prudence and courage, based on virtuous leadership and popular participation, can renew the promise of democracy. Martin Luther King, Jr., who was assassinated half a century ago, called it the noble purpose of making 'people . . . partners in power'.[4]

Notes

Introduction

1 For a critique of this narrative, see Jamie Bartlett, *The People vs Tech: How the Internet is Killing Democracy (and How We Save It)* (London: Ebury Press, 2018).

2 Edward Alden, *Failure to Adjust: How Americans Got Left Behind in the Global Economy* (Lanham, MD: Rowman & Littlefield, 2017); Edward Luce, *The Retreat of Western Liberalism* (London: Little, Brown, 2017).

3 Joan C. Williams, *White Working Class: Overcoming Class Cluelessness in America* (Boston: Harvard Business Review Press, 2017); Eric Kaufmann, *Whiteshift: Populism, Immigration and the Future of White Majorities* (London: Allen Lane, 2018).

4 Jeremy Cliffe, *Britain's Cosmopolitan Future: How the Country is Changing and Why its Politicians Must Respond*, 14 May 2015, www.policy-network.net/publications/4905/Britains-Cosmopolitan-Future; David Goodhart, *The Road to Somewhere: The New Tribes Shaping British* (London: Hurst, 2017).

5 This applies to the 'accelerationist' philosophy underpinning Marxist post-capitalism, e.g., Paul Mason,

Postcapitalism: A Guide to our Future (London: Allen Lane, 2015); Nick Srnicek and Alex Williams, *Inventing the Future: Postcapitalism and a World without Work* (London: Verso, 2015). For a longer critique, see my '"War of position": liberal interregnum and the emergent ideologies', *Telos*, no. 183 (summer 2018): 169–201.

6 Alain Supiot, *La Gouvernance par les nombres: cours au Collège de France, 2012–2014* (Paris: Fayard, 2015).

7 Mark Garnett, *The Snake that Swallowed its Tail: Some Contradictions in Modern Liberalism* (Exeter: Imprint Academic, 2004).

8 Here, as elsewhere in the book, I develop some arguments that arise from John Milbank and Adrian Pabst, *The Politics of Virtue: Post-Liberalism and the Human Future* (London: Rowman & Littlefield International, 2016), esp. pp. 13–67 and 179–244.

9 Michael Freeden, *The New Liberalism* (Oxford: Oxford University Press, 1978); Ellen Frankel Paul, Fred D. Miller and Jeffrey Paul (eds), *Liberalism: Old and New* (Cambridge: Cambridge University Press, 2007).

10 John Gray, 'The problem of hyper-liberalism', *Times Literary Supplement*, 30 March 2018, www.the-tls. co.uk/articles/public/john-gray-hyper-liberalism-liberty/.

11 Maurice Cowling, *Mill and Liberalism* (Cambridge: Cambridge University Press, 1963).

12 Dismissing illiberal democracy as a 'parody' and 'populist distortion' not only ignores a long tradition of thinking from Rousseau via Mill to Marx but also fails to acknowledge the popular rejection of undemocratic liberalism today. These omissions are a flaw in David Runciman's otherwise important book *How Democracy Ends* (London: Profile Books, 2018), p. 175.

13 Alexis de Tocqueville, *Democracy in America*, trans. G. Lawrence (New York: Doubleday, 1969), Vol. I, p. 650.

14 This downward spiral is absent from Yascha Mounk's *The People vs. Democracy: Why Our Freedom Is in Danger and How to Save It* (Cambridge, MA: Harvard University Press, 2018).

Chapter 1 Democracy between Liberalism and Populism

1 See 'Declining trust in government is denting democracy', 25 January 2017, www.economist.com/blogs/graph icdetail/2017/01/daily-chart-20; and *Freedom in the World 2018*, https://freedomhouse.org/sites/default/files/ FH_FITW_Report_2018_Final_SinglePage.pdf.

2 Larry Diamond, 'Facing up to the democratic recession', *Journal of Democracy*, 26/1 (2015): 141–55; Roberto Stefan Foa and Yascha Mounk, 'The democratic disconnect', *Journal of Democracy*, 27/3 (2016): 5–17, and 'The signs of deconsolidation', *Journal of Democracy*, 28/1 (2017): 5–15.

3 Ronald F. Inglehart, 'How much should we worry?', *Journal of Democracy*, 27/3 (2016): 18–23; see also contributions by Pippa Norris, Amy C. Alexander and Christian Wetzel to the *Journal of Democracy* Web Exchange, at www.journalofdemocracy.org/online-exc hange-"democratic-deconsolidation".

4 Joshua Kurlantzick, *Democracy in Retreat: The Revolt of the Middle Class and the Worldwide Decline of Representative Government* (New Haven, CT: Yale University Press, 2013), p. 83.

5 The most publicised and least persuasive statement of this myth of progress in our times is Steven Pinker's *Enlightenment Now: The Case for Reason, Science, Humanism, and Progress* (New York: Penguin, 2018).

6 See www.pewsocialtrends.org/2015/12/09/the-american-middle-class-is-losing-ground/; Richard V. Reeves, *Dream Hoarders: How the American Upper Middle*

Class is Leaving Everyone Else in the Dust, Why That is a Problem, and What to Do about It (Washington, DC: Brookings Institution, 2017).

7 Bernd Sommer, *Prekarisierung und Ressentiments: Soziale Unsicherheit und rechtsextreme Einstellungen in Deutschland* (Wiesbaden: VS Verlag, 2010); Laurent Bouvet, *L'insécurité culturelle: sortir du malaise identitaire français* (Paris: Fayard, 2015).

8 Peter Oborne, *The Triumph of the Political Class* (London: Simon & Schuster, 2007); Philip Coggan, *The Last Vote: The Threats to Western Democracy* (London: Allen Lane, 2013).

9 Anne Applebaum, 'Even if Trump loses, the "Populist International" wins', *Washington Post*, 7 November 2016; Nadia Marzouki, Duncan McDonnell and Olivier Roy (eds), *Saving the People: How Populists Hijack Religion* (London: Hurst, 2016); John Lloyd, 'The New Illiberal International', *New Statesman*, 18 July 2018, www.newstatesman.com/world/2018/07/new-illiberal-international.

10 Bill Emmott, *The Fate of the West: The Battle to Save the World's Most Successful Political Idea* (London: Profile Books, 2017); Edward Luce, *The Retreat of Western Liberalism* (London: Little, Brown, 2017).

11 Colin Crouch, *Post-Democracy* (Cambridge: Polity, 2004); Sheldon S. Wolin, *Democracy Incorporated: Managed Democracy and the Specter of Inverted Totalitarianism* (Princeton, NJ: Princeton University Press, 2008); Peter Mair, *Ruling the Void: The Hollowing-Out of Western Democracy* (London: Verso, 2013).

12 Steven Levitsky and Daniel Ziblatt, *How Democracies Die* (London: Viking, 2018); Yascha Mounk, *The People vs. Democracy* (Cambridge, MA: Harvard University Press, 2018); David Runciman, *How Democracy Ends* (London: Profile Books, 2018).

13 Mark Lilla, *The Once and Future Liberal: After Identity Politics* (New York: HarperCollins, 2017).

14 Anthony Barnett, 'Corporate populism and partyless democracy', *New Left Review*, 3 (May–June 2000): 80–9.

15 See again my '"War of position": liberal interregnum and the emergent ideologies', *Telos*, no. 183 (summer 2018): 169–201.

16 Thomas Raines, Matthew Goodwin and David Cutts, *The Future of Europe: Comparing Public and Elite Attitudes*, Research Paper, Chatham House, June 2017, www. chathamhouse.org/sites/files/chathamhouse/publications/ research/2017-06-20-future-europe-attitudes-raines-go odwin-cutts-final.pdf.

17 Tibor Fischer, 'I don't recognise Viktor Orbán as a "tyrant"', *The Guardian*, 20 April 2017, www.the guardian.com/commentisfree/2017/apr/20/viktor-orban-tyrant-western-media-hungarian-leader-democracy-antis emite.

18 John O'Sullivan, 'East vs West: the new battle for Europe', *The Spectator*, 27 January 2018, www.specta tor.co.uk/2018/01/the-fight-for-europe-is-now-between-east-and-west/.

19 Cas Mudde and Cristóbal Rovira Kaltwasser, *Populism: A Very Short Introduction* (Oxford: Oxford University Press, 2017), p. 116.

20 Pierre Manent, 'Populist demagogy and the fanaticism of the center', trans. Evelyn Flashner, *American Affairs*, 1/2 (2017): 9–18.

21 Kate Dommett, 'Post-democratic party politics', *Political Quarterly*, 87/1 (2016): 86–90.

22 Barnett, 'Corporate populism and partyless democracy', pp. 80–9; Russell J. Dalton and Martin P. Wattenberg (eds), *Parties without Partisans: Political Change in Advanced Industrial Democracies* (Oxford: Oxford University Press, 2002), pp. 261–85.

23 Richard Katz and Peter Mair, 'Changing models of party organization and party democracy: the emergence of the cartel party', *Party Politics*, 1/1 (1995): 5–28; Peter Mair, 'Partyless democracy: solving the paradox of New Labour', *New Left Review*, 2 (2000): 21–35.

24 Alexis de Tocqueville, *Democracy in America*, trans. G. Lawrence (New York: Doubleday, 1969), Vol. I, part 2, chap. 8, p. 266.

25 Ibid., p. 272.

26 Christopher Lasch, *The Revolt of the Elites and the Betrayal of Democracy* (New York: W. W. Norton, 1995); Paul Piccone, *Confronting the Crisis: Writings of Paul Piccone* (New York: Telos, 2008).

27 Isaiah Berlin, 'Two concepts of liberty', in *Four Essays on Liberty* (Oxford: Oxford University Press, 1969), pp. 118–72.

28 Giorgio Agamben, *State of Exception*, trans. Kevin Attell (Chicago: University of Chicago Press, 2005), pp. 1–40.

29 Evgeny Morozov, *To Save Everything, Click Here: Technology, Solutionism and the Urge to Fix Problems that Don't Exist* (London: Allen Lane, 2014); Jamie Bartlett, *The People vs Tech: How the Internet is Killing Democracy (and How We Save It)* (London: Ebury Press, 2018).

30 Michael J. Sandel, 'The procedural republic and the unencumbered self', *Political Theory*, 12/1 (1984): 81–96, at p. 94.

31 Robert Putnam, *Bowling Alone: The Collapse and Revival of American Community* (New York: Simon & Schuster, 2000); Theda Skocpol, *Diminished Democracy: From Membership to Management in American Civic Life* (Oklahoma City: University of Oklahoma Press, 2003).

32 Pierre Manent, *The City of Man*, trans. M. LePain (Princeton, NJ: Princeton University Press, 1998), p. 181.

33 Tocqueville, *Democracy in America*, Vol. I, p. 650.

Chapter 2 Oligarchy

1 Barry C. Lynn, *Cornered: The New Monopoly Capitalism and the Economics of Destruction* (Oxford: Wiley, 2010); Joshua Kurlantzick, *State Capitalism: How the Return of Statism is Transforming the World* (Oxford: Oxford University Press, 2016).

2 John Kay, *Other People's Money: Masters of the Universe or Servants of the People?* (London: Profile Books, 2015), pp. 80–140.

3 Brink Lindsey and Steven Teles, *The Captured Economy: How the Powerful Become Richer, Slow Down Growth, and Increase Inequality* (New York: Oxford University Press, 2017).

4 Rachel Reeves, *The Everyday Economy*, 22 March 2018, www.scribd.com/document/374425087/Rachel-Reeves-The-Everyday-Economy.

5 See Adrian Pabst, 'Political economy and the constitution of Europe's polity: pathways for the common currency beyond ordo-liberal and neo-functionalist models', in Ivano Cardinale, D'Maris Coffman and Roberto Scazzieri (eds), *The Political Economy of the Eurozone* (Cambridge: Cambridge University Press, 2017), pp. 183–215.

6 James Bloodworth, *Hired: Six Months Undercover in Low-Wage Britain* (London: Atlantic Books, 2018).

7 Oxfam, *Reward Work, not Wealth*, January 2018, https://d1tn3vj7xz9fdh.cloudfront.net/s3fs-public/file_attachments/bp-reward-work-not-wealth-220118-en.pdf.

8 Thomas Piketty, Emmanuel Saez and Gabriel Zucman, *Distributional National Accounts: methods and estimates for the United States*, NBER Working Paper no. 22945 (December 2016), www.nber.org/papers/w22945.

9 The Resolution Foundation Earnings Outlook Q4 2017,

www.resolutionfoundation.org/app/uploads/2018/03/Earnings-outlook-Q4-2017.pdf.

10 David Dayen, 'America's favorite monopolist: the shameful truth behind Warren Buffett's billions', *The Nation*, 12 March 2018, p. 18.

11 Karl Polanyi, *The Great Transformation: The Political and Economic Origins of Our Time* (Boston: Beacon Press, [1944] 2001).

12 Simcha Barkai, *Declining Labor and Capital Shares*, London Business School, 2017, http://facultyresearch. london.edu/docs/BarkaiDecliningLaborCapital.pdf.

13 John Lanchester, *Whoops! Why Everyone Owes Everyone and No One Can Pay* (London: Penguin, 2010).

14 'The big fight: interview of Sen. Elizabeth Warren with George Zornick', *The Nation*, 12 March 2018, p. 13.

15 Lynn, *Cornered*, p. 15.

16 Ibid., pp. 31–91.

17 Dayen, 'America's favorite monopolist', p. 16.

18 Ibid., p. 18.

19 Stacy Mitchell, 'The empire of everything', *The Nation*, 12 March 2018, p. 24.

20 Ibid. See also Olivia LaVecchia and Stacy Mitchell, *Amazon's Stranglehold: How the Company's Tightening Grip is Stifling Competition, Eroding Jobs, and Threatening Communities*, Institute for Local Self-Reliance, November 2016, https://ilsr.org/wp-content/uploads/2016/11/ILSR_AmazonReport_final.pdf.

21 Pew Research Center, 'The American middle class is losing ground', 9 December 2015, www.pewsocialtrends. org/2015/12/09/the-american-middle-class-is-losing-ground/.

22 Mitchell, 'The empire of everything', p. 25.

23 Lynn, *Cornered*, pp. 92–123.

24 Quoted ibid., p. 15.

25 Ibid., pp. 63–4. See Peter Drucker, *Concept of the Corporation* (New York: John Day, 1946).
26 Robert B. Reich, *The Work of Nations: Preparing Ourselves for 21st-Century Capitalism* (New York: Vintage, 1992), p. 3 (original emphasis).
27 Will Hutton, 'Capitalism's new crisis: after Carillion, can the private sector ever be trusted?', *The Observer*, 21 January 2018, www.theguardian.com/politics/2018/jan/21/capitalism-new-crisis-can-private-sector-be-trusted-carillion-privatisation?CMP=Share_iOSApp_Other.
28 Louis D. Brandeis, *Other People's Money, and How Bankers Use It* (New York: Frederick A. Stokes, 1914), p. 4.
29 Dayen, 'America's favorite monopolist', p. 32.
30 Alexis de Tocqueville, *Democracy in America*, trans. G. Lawrence (New York: Doubleday, 1969), Vol. I, p. 86.
31 Stefano Zamagni, 'Catholic social teaching, civil economy, and the spirit of capitalism', in Daniel K. Finn (ed.), *The True Wealth of Nations: Catholic Social Thought and Economic Life* (Oxford: Oxford University Press, 2010), p. 87.
32 Gary L. Reback, *Free the Market! Why Only Government Can Keep the Marketplace Competitive* (New York: Portfolio, 2009).
33 Robert Reich, *Saving Capitalism: For the Many, Not the Few* (New York: Penguin, 2015); Elizabeth Warren, 'America's monopoly moment: work, innovation, and control in an age of concentrated power', 6 December 2017, https://openmarketsinstitute.org/events/americas-monopoly-moment-work-innovation-and-control-in-an-age-of-concentrated-power/.
34 Mitchell, 'The empire of everything', p. 33.
35 Martin Schmalz, 'Warren Buffett is betting the airline oligopoly is here to stay', *Harvard Business Review*, 17

November 2016, https://hbr.org/2016/11/warren-buffett-is-betting-the-airline-oligopoly-is-here-to-stay.

36 Melanie Arntz, Terry Gregory and Ulrich Zierahn, *The Risk of Automation for Jobs in OECD Countries: A Comparative Analysis*, OECD Social, Employment and Migration Working Papers no. 189, 14 May 2016, www.oecd-ilibrary.org/docserver/download/5jlz9h56dvq7-en.pdf?expires=1491034458&id=id&accname=guest&checksum=3C8D94D490FEB91C2E8C1BB4BB4326FE.

37 GDP and similar measures fail to capture innovation, services and intangible goods, as well as all the relational goods we hold in common. See Diane Coyle, *GDP: A Brief but Affectionate History* (Princeton, NJ: Princeton University Press, 2015); David Pilling, *The Growth Delusion: The Wealth and Well-Being of Nations* (London: Bloomsbury, 2018).

38 Colin Mayer, *Firm Commitment: Why the Corporation is Failing Us and How to Restore Trust in It* (Oxford: Oxford University Press, 2013), pp. 117–57.

Chapter 3 Demagogy

1 John Rawls, *A Theory of Justice* (Cambridge, MA: Harvard University Press, 1971); Jürgen Habermas, *Postmetaphysical Thinking: Between Metaphysics and the Critique of Reason*, trans. W. M. Hohengarten (Cambridge: Polity, 1995).

2 Benjamin Constant, 'The liberty of the ancients compared with that of the moderns', in *Constant: Political Writings*, ed. Biancamaria Fontana (Cambridge: Cambridge University Press, 1988), pp. 308–28.

3 Isaiah Berlin, 'Two concepts of liberty', in *Four Essays on Liberty* (Oxford: Oxford University Press, 1969), pp. 118–72.

4 Zygmunt Bauman, *Does Ethics Have a Chance in a World*

of Consumers? (Cambridge, MA: Harvard University Press, 2008), p. 72.

5 C. B. Macpherson, *The Political Theory of Possessive Individualism: Hobbes to Locke* (Oxford: Clarendon Press, 1962).

6 Louis Dupré, *Passage to Modernity: An Essay in the Hermeneutics of Nature and Culture* (New Haven, CT: Yale University Press, 1993).

7 Marshall Sahlins, *The Western Illusion of Human Nature* (Chicago: Prickly Paradigm Press, 2008).

8 Jean-Claude Michéa, *L'Empire du moindre mal: essai sur la civilisation libérale* (Paris: Climats, 2007); trans. David Fernbach as *The Realm of Lesser Evil: An Essay on Liberal Civilisation* (Cambridge: Polity, 2009).

9 Mark Lilla, 'The end of identity liberalism', *New York Times*, 18 November 2016, www.nytimes.com/2016/11/20/opinion/sunday/the-end-of-identity-liberalism.html?_r=0; expanded as *The Once and Future Liberal: After Identity Politics* (New York: HarperCollins, 2017).

10 See Christopher Lasch, *The Agony of the American Left* (New York: Knopf, 1969); *Haven in a Heartless World: The Family Besieged* (New York: W. W. Norton, 1977); *The Culture of Narcissism: American Life in an Age of Diminishing Expectations* (New York: W. W. Norton, 1979).

11 Ross Douthat, 'The crisis for liberalism', *New York Times*, 19 November 2016, www.nytimes.com/2016/11/20/opinion/sunday/the-crisis-for-liberalism.html.

12 This section draws on my '"War of position": liberal interregnum and the emergent ideologies', *Telos*, no. 183 (summer 2018): 169–201.

13 David Neiwert, *Alt-America: The Rise of the Radical Right in the Age of Trump* (London: Verso, 2017); Paul

Stocker, *English Uprising: Brexit and the Mainstreaming of the Far Right* (London: Melville House, 2017).

14 Nick Srnicek and Alex Williams, *Inventing the Future: Postcapitalism and a World without Work* (London: Verso, 2015); Paul Mason, *Postcapitalism: A Guide to our Future* (London: Allen Lane, 2015); Aaron Bastani, *Fully Automated Luxury Communism: A Manifesto* (London: Verso, 2019).

15 John Gray, 'The Power and the Story: fact, fabrication and the shaping of the modern media – a review of John Lloyd's book *The Power and the Story*', *New Statesman*, 14 August 2017, www.newstatesman.com/culture/books/2017/08/power-and-story-fact-fabrication-and-shaping-modern-media.

16 Joan C. Williams, *White Working Class: Overcoming Class Cluelessness in America* (Boston: Harvard Business Review Press, 2017); Joshua Kurlantzick, *Democracy in Retreat: The Revolt of the Middle Class and the Worldwide Decline of Representative Government* (New Haven, CT: Yale University Press, 2013).

17 Matthew d'Ancona, *Post-Truth: The New War on Truth and How to Fight Back* (London: Ebury Press, 2017), p. 119.

18 Alasdair MacIntyre, *After Virtue: A Study in Moral Theory* (3rd edn, London: Duckworth, 2000).

19 Harry G. Frankfurt, *On Bullshit* (Princeton, NJ: Princeton University Press, 2005).

20 James Ball, *Post-Truth: How Bullshit Conquered the World* (London: Biteback, 2017).

21 As John Lanchester writes, 'in 2015 musicians earned less from it [YouTube] and from its ad-supported rivals than they earned from sales of vinyl. Not CDs and recordings in general: vinyl', in 'You are the product', *London Review of Books*, 17 August 2017, pp. 3–10, www.lrb.co.uk/v39/n16/john-lanchester/you-are-the-product.

22 Jonathan Taplin, *Move Fast and Break Things: How Facebook, Google and Amazon have Cornered Culture and What it Means for All of Us* (London: Macmillan, 2017), p. 206.

23 Tom Wu, *The Attention Merchants: From the Daily Newspaper to Social Media, How Our Time and Attention is Harvested and Sold* (London: Atlantic Books, 2017).

24 Quoted in Lanchester, 'You are the product' (emphasis added).

25 Ibid.

26 Seth Stephens-Davidowitz, *Everybody Lies: Big Data, New Data, and What the Internet Can Tell Us about Who We Really Are* (New York: Dey Street, 2017).

27 Jamie Bartlett, 'Big data is watching you – and it wants your vote', *The Spectator*, 24 March 2018, www.spec tator.co.uk/2018/03/big-data-is-watching-you-and-it-wa nts-your-vote/.

28 For my critique of Bernard Williams's *Truth and Truthfulness* (Princeton, NJ: Princeton University Press, 2004), see my article '"A habitual disposition to the good": on reason, virtue and realism', *Global Discourse*, 5/2 (2015): 261–79.

29 Charles Taylor, *Modern Social Imaginaries* (Durham, NC: Duke University Press, 2004), p. 23.

Chapter 4 Anarchy

1 John Milbank and Adrian Pabst, *The Politics of Virtue: Post-Liberalism and the Human Future* (London: Rowman & Littlefield International, 2016), pp. 179–204.

2 Peter Mair, *Ruling the Void: The Hollowing-Out of Western Democracy* (London: Verso, 2013).

3 Robert Putnam, *Bowling Alone: The Collapse and Revival of American Community* (New York: Simon & Schuster, 2000); Theda Skocpol, *Diminished Democracy:*

From Membership to Management in American Civic Life (Oklahoma City: University of Oklahoma Press, 2003).

4 Richard Robison (ed.), *The Neo-Liberal Revolution: Forging the Market State* (Basingstoke: Palgrave Macmillan, 2006).

5 Philip Bobbitt, *The Shield of Achilles: War, Peace and the Course of History* (London: Penguin, 2003), pp. 213–42, quotes at pp. 234–5.

6 Karl Polanyi, *The Great Transformation: The Political and Economic Origins of Our Time* (Boston: Beacon Press, [1944] 2001).

7 Nancy Fraser, 'A triple movement? Parsing the politics of crisis after Polanyi', *New Left Review*, 81 (2013): 119–32.

8 Rachel Reeves, 'Throwing a new light on loneliness', speech hosted by Policy Exchange, 11 December 2017, https://policyexchange.org.uk/pxevents/rachel-reeves-mp-throwing-a-new-light-on-loneliness/.

9 Sherry Turkle, *Alone Together: Why We Expect More from Technology and Less from Each Other* (London: Hachette, 2011); *Reclaiming Conversation: The Power of Talk in a Digital Age* (New York: Penguin, 2015).

10 Jean-Claude Michéa, *L'Empire du moindre mal: essai sur la civilisation libérale* (Paris: Climats, 2007); trans. David Fernbach as *The Realm of Lesser Evil: An Essay on Liberal Civilisation* (Cambridge: Polity, 2009).

11 For a longer exposition of this argument, see Milbank and Pabst, *The Politics of Virtue*, pp. 13–67.

12 Serge Latouche, *L'Invention de l'économie* (Paris: Albin Michel, 2005), esp. pp. 154–60.

13 Jean Rohou, *Le XVIIe Siècle: une révolution de la condition humaine* (Paris: Seuil, 2002).

14 Michéa, *The Realm of Lesser Evil*.

15 John Rawls, *A Theory of Justice* (Cambridge, MA: Harvard University Press, 1971); Ronald Dworkin,

Taking Rights Seriously (Cambridge, MA: Harvard University Press, 1977).

16 Friedrich von Hayek, 'The principles of a liberal social order', in *Studies in Philosophy, Politics and Economics* (London: Routledge & Kegan Paul, 1967), pp. 160–77.

17 Alexis de Tocqueville, *Democracy in America*, trans. George Lawrence (New York: HarperCollins, 2000), p. 109.

18 Paul Hirst, *Associative Democracy: New Forms of Economic and Social Governance* (Cambridge: Polity, 1996); Paul Hirst and Veit-Michael Bader (eds), *Associative Democracy: The Real Third Way* (London: Frank Cass, 2001).

19 Among the key thinkers are Pierre-Joseph Proudhon, Robert Owen, George Jacob Holyoake, John Neville Figgis, Harold J. Laski and G. D. H. Cole. See Paul Hirst (ed.), *The Pluralist Theory of the State: Selected Writings of G. D. H. Cole, J. N. Figgis and H. J. Laski* (London: Routledge, 1989).

20 Polanyi, *The Great Transformation*, pp. 140–71.

21 Paul Hirst, *From Statism to Pluralism: Democracy, Civil Society and Global Politics* (London: Routledge, 1997), p. 32.

22 Michael Freeden, *The New Liberalism* (Oxford: Oxford University Press, 1978).

23 Maurice Glasman, 'How to combine Hirst and Polanyi to create a strong argument for an embedded and democratic economy', in Andrea Westall (ed.), *Revisiting Associative Democracy: How to Get More Co-operation, Co-ordination and Collaboration into our Economy, our Democracy, our Public Services, and our Lives* (London: Lawrence & Wishart, 2011), p. 69.

24 Jane Wills, *Locating Localism: Statecraft, Citizenship and Democracy* (Bristol: Policy Press, 2016).

25 Hilary Cottam, *Radical Help: How We Can Remake the Relationships between Us and Revolutionise the Welfare State* (London: Virago, 2018).

26 Maurice Glasman, lecture delivered at the University of Kent, 31 January 2018.

27 I have argued elsewhere for the introduction of a national civic service. See Adrian Pabst, *A Common Good Approach to Free Movement and Capital*, with a foreword by Rachel Reeves MP (London: St Paul's Institute, 2018), www.stpaulsinstitute.org.uk/assets/images/sp_co mmongoodapproachtofreemovement.pdf.

Chapter 5 Tyranny

1 Alain Supiot, *La Gouvernance par les nombres: cours au Collège de France, 2012–2014* (Paris: Fayard, 2015).

2 For an early statement of the anti-humanist tyranny of managerial revolution, see James Burnham, *The Managerial Revolution: What is Happening in the World* (New York: John Day, 1942).

3 Stephen Toulmin, *Cosmopolis: The Hidden Agenda of Modernity* (Chicago: University of Chicago Press, 1990).

4 Eric Voegelin, *The New Science of Politics* (Chicago: University of Chicago Press, 1952).

5 Raymond Aron, *Essai sur les libertés* (Paris: Calman-Lévy, 1965); trans. Helen Weaver as *An Essay on Freedom* (New York: World, 1970).

6 Danny Kruger, *On Fraternity: Politics beyond Liberty and Equality* (London: Institute for the Study of Civil Society, 2007), p. 47.

7 Aron, *Essai sur les libertés*, p. 211 (my translation).

8 Michael Hardt and Antonio Negri, *Multitude: War and Democracy in the Age of Empire* (London: Penguin,

2005); Nick Srnicek and Alex Williams, *Inventing the Future: Postcapitalism and a World without Work* (London: Verso, 2015); Paul Mason, *Postcapitalism: A Guide to our Future* (London: Allen Lane, 2015).

9 Steven Pinker, *Enlightenment Now: The Case for Reason, Science, Humanism, and Progress* (New York: Penguin, 2018).

10 John Gray, *Enlightenment's Wake: Politics and Culture at the Close of the Modern Age* (London: Routledge, 1995); *Heresies: Against Progress and Other Illusions* (London: Granta, 2004).

11 Nick Land, the father of 'accelerationism', which informs both left- and right-wing libertarians, is the author of *The Thirst for Annihilation: Georges Bataille and Virulent Nihilism* (London: Routledge, 1992) and *The Dark Enlightenment* (2013), www.thedarkenlightenment.com/the-dark-enlightenment-by-nick-land/.

12 Ray Brassier, 'Prometheanism and its critics', in Robin Mackay and Armen Avenessian (eds), *#Accelerate: The Accelerationist Reader* (Falmouth: Urbanomic, 2014), pp. 467–88.

13 Ray Brassier, *Nihil Unbound: Enlightenment and Extinction* (London: Palgrave Macmillan, 2007), p. ix.

14 Alex Williams and Nick Srnicek, '#Accelerate: manifesto for an accelerationist politics', in Mackay and Avenessian, *#Accelerate*, pp. 347–62.

15 Sherry Turkle, *Alone Together: Why We Expect More from Technology and Less from Each Other* (London: Hachette, 2011).

16 Tony Anatrella, *Le Règne de Narcisse: les enjeux du déni de la différence sexuelle* (Paris: Presses de la Renaissance, 2005).

17 Aaron Bastani, *Fully Automated Luxury Communism: A Manifesto* (London: Verso, 2019).

18 Jon Cruddas, 'The humanist left must challenge the rise

of cyborg socialism', *New Statesman*, 23 April 2018, www.newstatesman.com/politics/uk/2018/04/humanist-left-must-challenge-rise-cyborg-socialism.

19 David Neiwert, *Alt-America: The Rise of the Radical Right in the Age of Trump* (London: Verso, 2017).

20 Jonathan Taplin, *Move Fast and Break Things: How Facebook, Google and Amazon have Cornered Culture and What it Means for All of Us* (London: Macmillan, 2017).

21 William Davies, *The Happiness Industry: How Government and Big Business Sold Us Well-Being* (London: Verso, 2015).

22 C. B. Macpherson, *The Political Theory of Possessive Individualism: Hobbes to Locke* (Oxford: Clarendon Press, 1962).

23 Patrick J. Deneen, *Why Liberalism Failed* (New Haven, CT: Yale University Press, 2018).

24 Peter Singer, *Unsanctifying Human Life: Essays on Ethics* (Oxford: Blackwell, 2002), p. 225.

25 Sylviane Agacinski, *Corps en miettes* (rev. edn, Paris: Flammarion, 2013); Muriel Fabre-Magnan, *La Gestation pour autrui: fictions et réalité* (Paris: Fayard, 2013).

Conclusion

1 Fareed Zakaria, 'The rise of illiberal democracy', *Foreign Affairs*, 76 (November–December 1997): 22–43.

2 Edmund Burke, *Reflections on the Revolution in France* (1790), in *Burke: Revolutionary Writings*, ed. Ian Hampsher-Monk (Cambridge: Cambridge University Press, 2014), p. 101.

3 David Miller, *Strangers in Our Midst: The Political Philosophy of Immigration* (Cambridge, MA: Harvard University Press, 2016).

4 Martin Luther King, Jr., 'Where do we go from here?', in *A*

Testament of Hope: The Essential Writings and Speeches of Martin Luther King, Jr., ed. James M. Washington (New York: HarperCollins, 1986), p. 586.

Index

Index

Index

Index

Index

Index

Index

Index

Index

Index

Index

Index

portable data 63
post-capitalism 4, 83, 153–4n5
post-Cold War 11, 34
post-democracy 15, 26, 100–5
post-human species 136
post-liberalism 4
post-modernism 4, 86
post-truth 74, 77, 84, 85–6
Poujadisme 29
poverty 13, 51, 104, 122
power
  capitalism 38–9
  centralised 102, 108
  cultural redistribution of
    133
  devolved 117–19
  distribution 134
  ethos 93–9
  executive/citizens 31
  labour/capital 54, 66
  mixed government 124–5
  rentiers 36
  tech platforms 90, 91
  Tocqueville 59
precarious employment 36–7,
  51
price factors 39–40, 48, 54
privacy 30, 91–2
privatisation 55, 103
Procter & Gamble 45
professional class 24, 42–3,
  58–9, 67, 81
profits 40, 41–2, 44, 50, 70
progress
  Enlightenment 137, 139
  faith in 5, 6
  historicism 130
  Pinker 155n5
  reversible 137
  stalled 12–13
Project Fear 17, 87
Prometheanism 138, 139,
  143–4
propaganda 1, 91, 95
protectionism 83–4

Proudhon, Pierre-Joseph
  167n19
public opinion 16, 28–9, 77,
  86–7, 95
public works programmes 70

race factors 20, 73, 141–2
railways 41–2, 53, 63
Rassemblement National 12
rationality/reason 74, 78, 137
Rawls, John 27, 74, 111, 132
Reagan, Ronald 55, 60
reciprocity 8, 9, 101, 122, 133
recognition: *see* mutual
  recognition
Reeves, Rachel 36
regional assemblies 121–2
Reich, Robert 56, 61, 161n33
relationships
  civic associations 6
  liberalism 145
  mutualism 114
  ordering of 28
  real-life 4, 91, 92, 106, 134,
    140–1, 151–2
  reciprocity 8, 101
  release from 139
  shared interests 122
  as transactions 39
  trust 120
  virtue 124
  see also family bonds;
    fragmentation of society
religious fundamentalists 73
rent extraction 47, 48, 57
rentier economy 36, 52–9
representation 25–6, 97, 119,
  132
La République en Marche 13
Resolution Foundation 38
responsibilities 71, 96, 101,
  113, 117, 126
right to reply 97
rights
  duties 7–8, 113

184

Index

Index

Index

Index

188